AN IMPORTANT MESSAGE FROM RANDY

This is the page where you would normally find testimonials from influential people who have read an advance draft of the manuscript. I have chosen not to include any in this book. This subject matter will be controversial for many and frightening for some. Field leaders may be hesitant to publicly endorse the book, because they could face repercussions from their corporate team or even renegade factions in their own team. Likewise, some company owners and executives might be fearful that their field leaders could feel threatened by what this book reveals. The man behind the curtain usually doesn't want you to know he's behind the curtain.

Although some courageous leaders have offered to provide quotes, I wasn't comfortable accepting their generous offers. This book will end the careers of some people in our business. And provide the last nail in the coffin for some companies— rightly so. But this book will also be a catalyst to ignite the careers for the next generation of empowering leaders in our business. And perhaps birth the next great companies.

This is a book for a small but impactful subsection of the profession: the leaders (both field and corporate) with the power to change the game. It's a book that will cause significant collateral damage to the negative forces in our profession and they won't take it lightly. They will attack with all they have left. I don't want to put anyone else in that line of attack. I will face it alone because I believe in the profession as perhaps no one else does. And I believe in you.

—RG

DEFCON 1
DIRECT SELLING

DEFCON 1
DIRECT SELLING

New York Times Bestselling Author

RANDY GAGE

MANUAL FOR FIELD LEADERS

WILEY

Published by John Wiley & Sons, Inc., Hoboken, New Jersey.

Published simultaneously in Canada.

For general information on our other products and services or for technical support, please contact our Customer Care Department within the United States at (800) 762-2974, outside the United States at (317) 572-3993 or fax (317) 572-4002.

Wiley publishes in a variety of print and electronic formats and by print-on-demand. Some material included with standard print versions of this book may not be included in e-books or in print-on-demand. If this book refers to media such as a CD or DVD that is not included in the version you purchased, you may download this material at http://booksupport.wiley.com. For more information about Wiley products, visit www.wiley.com.

Library of Congress Cataloging-in-Publication Data:

ISBN 9781119642114 (Paperback)
ISBN 9781119642091 (ePDF)
ISBN 9781119642121 (ePub)

Cover image: © Samarskaya/Getty Images
Cover design: Wiley

Printed in the United States of America

10 9 8 7 6 5 4 3 2 1

This book is dedicated to the worst sponsor I ever had. You don't even know who you are, but I'll never forget you. And know that because you were weak, I grew strong.

Contents

INTRODUCTION
LIVING THE ~~NIGHTMARE~~ DREAM...

The car was a '71 Plymouth Satellite, a pretty sweet ride when it first rolled off the assembly line in Detroit. I managed to buy it in 1979 for $1,500, because my mom co-signed the note and I arranged to finance it over three years. But by the time I was driving it to opportunity meetings in 1980, it already qualified as a broke-mobile.

I always parked in the back reaches of the hotel parking lot or by the loading dock. I would be meeting prospects at the meetings to show them how they could "live the dream," and I didn't want them to realize they probably had more money than I did.

But here's the craziest part of all that. If you had asked me then whether I would be releasing a book in 2020, distilling the secrets of my success and leadership in Direct Selling, I would have said, "Of course."

Probably not what you thought I was going to say. And if you did hear my answer back then, you probably would have thought I was irrational, foolish, and naive. And you'd have been right.

AND THAT'S WHY I CAN ACTUALLY WRITE THIS BOOK

And that's why you can read it with confidence, knowing it can help *you* be irrational, foolish, and naive too. Irrational, foolish, and naive enough to live your dreams. Because the number of rational, wise, and skeptical people in the world who are living their dreams would probably fit in a subway car.

My story really is one of those romantic, "rags to riches" tales that we all love to hear. A kid who was expelled from high school and served time for armed robbery—who was able to transform his life to become happy, successful, and wealthy. However, too often these stories of transformation leave out the messy middle stages, the drama and trauma that have to be endured and persevered through to reach the "lived happily ever after" ending.

Not this field manual.

This is the book that some wish you would never see or know about. The people who don't want you to read it fear that what you're about to discover might scare you away. Might blow up the idealistic narrative they're trying to sell you.

BUT I WANT YOU TO KNOW THE TRUTH

The truth that, yes, you can be successful, build a large team, and live your dreams. But also the truth that it is going to take real work, dedication, and endless endurance—and that you'll need more than just goals and a positive attitude. You'll need an actual game plan. And most importantly, the truth that growing your business won't always go according to your game plan. That sometimes your game plan is going to get blown out of the water, and you're going to have to suck it up and create a new one.

I SEE DEAD PEOPLE

And by dead people, I mean clueless people in a coma of delusion. The people in charge of "the system." The system that says go $80,000 or $100,000 in debt for a college degree that is out of date before you even graduate, then sell your soul to a series of jobs you don't like or actually hate, trading hours for money in the hopes of financially existing with your head barely above water. And doing this for 40 or 50 years to "retire" in a position of still needing financial supplementation to get by.

I think we've lost the plot....

Do we really have to work six days a week to enjoy one off? Work 50 weeks a year to vacation for two? We have an education system now that is preparing people to be worker drones in the collective. Entitlement mentality is running amok and we've forgotten what it means to live a life of meaning. There is nothing wrong with working a job for a salary, getting paid a fair wage for an honest effort. We all must start someplace, whether that is working a drive-thru, scrubbing bathrooms, or washing dishes in a pancake house like I did. But let's not become immune to the opportunity of developing and progressing, becoming the highest possible version of ourselves in everything we do, including our career.

Entrepreneurship is not for everyone. I get that. But there are millions of people in unfulfilling jobs for whom an entrepreneurial opportunity would provide a much better alternative. And these people don't realize that opportunity is available to them because they have bought into the "normalcy" of the current system. With this field manual, I'm going to show you exactly how you can best share this opportunity with them. Not with high-pressure sales techniques or hype, but by truly educating your candidates about the possibilities you can offer them.

It's not your job to sponsor everyone you know. But it is your job to offer people what you have, allow them to self-select in or out, and then help those who decide to join you.

Make the commitment now that this is the culture you will create on your team. Don't "close" people; "open" them to the possibilities.

The insights you discover in this book are meant to equip you for the dirty realities you will confront and to demonstrate to you that you're not the first person to face such daunting circumstances. Every great leader must face down extraordinary challenges before they come out victorious on the other side.

Please allow me to share with you how this book came about.

It was January 2019 and I was doing the final edits on my most recent book, *Direct Selling Success*. I sent proof copies to more than 20 top income earners in various companies to get their input. It immediately became apparent that the book would be a worldwide smash, an international bestseller. To a person, these leaders wanted to know how soon it would be published, whether they could share key sections with their top leaders, and whether I would give them permission to begin training sessions based on the content.

And Then Something Fascinating Occurred

For three days straight I received urgent messages from three of those leaders who had read select chapters of the book. Now they were seeking help with a burning situation that had arisen with their teams. They each were desperate to know if I had additional advice that could apply to their unique situations.

In each of these cases, the leader and their team faced a "DEFCON 1" type of situation. The DEFCON scale (short for "Defense Readiness Condition") measures the alert level of defense forces. DEFCON 1 is the maximum level status, used to describe preparation for imminent nuclear war. Obviously, these leaders were not facing anything close to an actual war. But they were facing exceptional, crisis scenarios that threatened the ongoing existence of their business.

In one case, a lot of their top leaders had lost confidence in the company and left en masse to join another one. In another case, the company had made major changes to the comp plan, and the results were causing a huge drop in volume and lots of resignations. In the third case, many leaders had been influenced by an outside generic trainer who had taught them systems that were actually eroding their businesses. These three leaders needed to act fast, or they would lose their teams and their livelihoods. If you develop a large team, at some point you too will face a "DEFCON 1" type of scenario for your business.

AND THAT'S WHY I'M WRITING THIS NEW BOOK

Here's the thing about leadership, particularly in Direct Selling. (For most of this book, I will refer to this as Leveraged Sales, which I believe is a much more appropriate label for this business model.) Most people believe leadership is about being positive all the time, sending out lots of happy, smiley emojis in their WhatsApp groups, and always giving positive motivational speeches. But the truth is, that's not leadership—that's propaganda. Well-meaning propaganda, surely, but propaganda nonetheless. And you're going to have to do better than that.

That's not to say there is no place for the "moonbeams, unicorns, and rainbows" perspective in leadership. There most certainly is. But that positive, optimistic, motivational outlook is only *one* element of leadership.

BECAUSE TRUE LEADERSHIP DEALS WITH THE MESSY, COMPLICATED, AND DARK AREAS AS WELL

How do you stay true to your principles and lead the team forward when their world is falling apart because of a comp plan change, regulatory attacks, or a competitor poaching away top leaders? Or when 90 percent of the product line is on backorder, the company can't make commissions, or there's a sociopath in the sponsorship line above you? You're going to need to exercise a higher level of leadership. One that reflects the yin and yang dichotomy of leading in the real world.

Here's how I define leadership in our space:

Inspiring people to become the highest possible version of themselves—and building the environment that facilitates this process.

And to do that, you can't just play the "only happy news" channel; you can't just be the positive, motivational "I did it, you can do this too" channel. Your people require more from you. A lot more.

This book you are reading now is the brutal, unvarnished truth about leadership. A book like no one has ever written before. Because it is a manual for field leaders on how to handle the most challenging elements of the Leveraged Sales business. I will share with you everything I have learned over almost four decades of leading huge teams all over the world.

I'm going to reveal the entire panorama of leadership—the joyful empowering moments and the messy, discouraging ones. I'll give you case studies and examples of my best leadership success—and lay bare my foolish, vain, and destructive mistakes as well.

A note of warning: A lot of my work is family friendly. But in my private coaching sessions and strategy sessions with my top leaders, my language is raw and uncensored (which is a nice way to say I swear a lot). Because this is meant to be a field manual for use in the most urgent and threatening emergencies and crisis situations, I'm not sugarcoating anything. So if profanity offends your sensibilities, this may not be the right book for you.

ONE OF THE MOST IMPORTANT LEADERSHIP SKILLS IS THE ABILITY TO TELL THE TRUTH

And to tell that truth with love and compassion and empathy, but truth nonetheless.

This book is a demonstration of my modeling that behavior for you. By the time your organization grows large, bad things are sometimes going to happen. Your company will make mistakes, your sponsorship line will make mistakes, other people in the profession will make mistakes, and you, yes you, will make mistakes.

There are no great leaders who don't make mistakes. That's only in the movies. In the real world, leadership is about recognizing, acknowledging, and owning your mistakes. And when the mistakes do happen, it's about not trying to gloss them over, not hiding them from the team, but to concede them and explain:

How they happened, why they happened, and why they won't happen again.

Regardless of who makes the mistakes, they will happen, and you are going to sometimes face those DEFCON 1 scenarios. It won't matter who caused them, only how you handle those situations—drawing on your resilience, tenacity, and character to show your team you have the ability to lead them.

I wrote this book to guide you through the process of developing that resilience, tenacity, and character. And also to provide you with some background on the little-known, inside workings of our profession, the critical-thinking skills necessary to adapt to chaotic circumstances, and the wisdom to make right choices.

You'll quickly notice I'm not starting the book with how you manage all the crisis, DEFCON 1 scenarios you are likely to face. Because the best way to handle an emergency is by preventing it from happening to begin with.

So the first chapters are about the principles you can follow, the culture you can create, and the behavior you can model that actually reduce the number of emergency situations requiring your leadership intervention. But of course, you're still going to encounter some negative situations that are unpreventable. And the second part of this book will prepare you for resolving them in the best ways possible.

If you're up for that, let's get after it.

—Randy Gage
Miami Beach, Florida
February 2020

CHAPTER 1

It's All on You

On the lovely island of Maui, with tall palm trees swaying in the breeze, I lounged poolside, working on my tan while my teammates engaged in a fierce water polo match. (And yes, literally drinking out of a coconut.) It was an incentive trip for top leaders to celebrate and reward us for another stellar year of performance. I was serenely reading a book when Jeremiah, one of the company VPs, interrupted my bliss with the news.

He relayed that he had just received a call telling him that my then-sponsor was about to jump to another company. At that very moment my sponsor—whom the company had flown to the island first class and lavished with swag, perks, excursions, and an oceanfront suite—was in that very oceanfront suite, dialing for dollars to take people to his next deal. And planning to tell me the following day.

I gazed at Jeremiah thoughtfully for a very long time. Then, sighing heavily, I said, "You know, some days I hate this goddamned job."

I had every right to feel appalled, disappointed, and betrayed. It would have been easy for me to slip into martyr mode and seek commiseration for the injustice inflicted upon me. But here's the reality...

THE PERSON MOST RESPONSIBLE FOR THIS TURN OF EVENTS WAS ME

Because I had failed in my job as a leader to protect my people and create a safe environment for them. I had initially embraced this man and sponsored under him because I chose to believe that he had become the new person he assured me he was, not the person reflected by the track record he had of moving from company to company over the years.

BUT HERE'S WHERE I HAD REALLY FALLEN DOWN

I had edified my sponsor, shared the platform with him, and facilitated his face being seen as a leader of our organization and company. By doing this, I had placed my team in a position of vulnerability. I had created a system and a culture that presented this person as a credible component of our support structure and a powerful resource for building their business.

Now team members would wake up the next day to discover that someone they had perceived as an asset had essentially become a threat. (Please don't read this as my suggesting my sponsor was an evil, diabolical villain, looking to attack and hurt others; he wasn't. He had simply made a decision he believed offered the best choice for his future success and security. One that now conflicted with the status to which I had played a part in elevating him.)

The whole sad scenario was no one's fault but my own. Years earlier I had made an expedient choice without thinking about the long-term potential consequences, and now the bill was coming due.

How Behavior Is Changed

Austrian economist Ludwig von Mises is acknowledged as one of the leaders in praxeology, the study of human action. (And what could possibly be more relevant to leadership in our profession than the study of why humans act as they do?) Herr von Mises developed the concept that getting humans to make a change in behavior requires three steps:

1. They are dissatisfied with their current state.
2. They have a vision of a better state.
3. They can see a path to get there.

As a leader in Leveraged Sales, you must understand these three steps with every fiber of your being. The key step is your ability to show you know the right path to get people where they want to go.

Here's the Hardest Part...

Applying the lesson to yourself. Meaning, instead of waiting for someone else to lead, you choose yourself to lead. Recognizing that you don't like your current state, visualizing what your ideal state would be, and then mapping out a path to get there. Which is another way of stating that leading others always begins with leading yourself.

Another Example of Poor Decision-Making and Leadership on My Part

Since I'm in confession mode, let me share another story. A year or two before that Hawaiian holiday, one of my top leaders left to try his luck with another company.

The reason he left is that he felt like he was a failure. He couldn't figure out what he was doing wrong and thought maybe a change of scenery or sponsor would help him discover what he was missing.

Here's the Thing

He had a large, growing team and was earning more than $50,000 a month. Yet he felt he wasn't measuring up. Why? Because I was earning about $120,000 a month and that's the standard he was using to measure his own success.

Once again, it would have been easy for me to slip into victim mode and lament as to why he would leave me. But there's no doubt in my mind that I lost him because I wasn't a strong enough leader. It's apparent that I had created a culture where someone earning 50K a month didn't feel recognized, valued, or successful.

That's totally on me. And when these kinds of dramatic developments happen in your organization— the good ones and the bad ones—they are totally on you.

OWN THE PROBLEM

This is the stunning truth about leadership: Whatever the problem is, it is always *your* problem, even when the situation is not your fault nor created by you. As a leader, you have to be the first and last line of defense for your team, protecting them from anything that will distract, weaken, or harm them. That doesn't mean this is fair, because often it's not. But that's why we get the big bucks.

If you're not willing to work through this reality, then leadership in Leveraged Sales is certainly not for you.

Think of your role this way: You must be the buffer between your team and everyone and everything that comes between them and their potential success.

Your team has the ability to rise to strong levels of resilience, tenacity, and effort. But these traits will only be made manifest if the team is led in the proper manner.

Five Frequent Mistakes

Here are five of the most frequent mistakes I see being made in leadership strategy when leaders face a DEFCON 1 scenario:

1) Let's Pretend This Isn't Happening

This is simply a case of wishful, delusional thinking. The premise of this line of thought (delusion) is that maybe the field won't realize something bad is going down. Something horrible happens, whether it's a scandal with the CEO or a logistical breakdown, and the leadership thinks that if they don't talk about it, no one will notice.

I flew on the Concorde a couple times, traveling Mach 2.2, and I can assure you that it didn't travel as fast as gossip does in your organization. The very bleak news you're hoping many people don't know about has probably already been shared on Instagram 459 times. (Or soon will be.) And when you don't acknowledge this problem reality, people get very suspicious, very quickly. The result becomes the team believing you don't have sufficient intelligence and awareness to understand what really goes on. Not a very inspiring way to lead a team.

2) Let's Keep This a Secret

This is an even worse alternative to mistake number one. There's a cliché in politics that was coined during the Watergate scandal: the coverup is worse than the crime. And it is just as appropriate in Leveraged Sales.

Why this mistake is even worse than mistake number one is because now duplicity is apparent. Secrets always get out. And the fact that you knew about this secret and tried to cover it up is extremely damaging, because most likely you lose credibility with your team and they no longer trust you. This is one of the quickest ways to kill team morale and forward momentum. (Or even kill a team.)

3) Let's Launch a "Distract Attack"

They say the best defense is a good offense. And sometimes that's true. And a lot of the time it's not. This is an old ruse long used by governments. Companies frequently attempt to employ this technique as well. Example: Sales are tanking, recruiting is dying, and a large number of distributors are quitting. Instead of identifying the cause and working to correct it, the company starts a campaign to attack a competitor company, hoping to distract the field from the issues at hand. Distractions work temporarily, but when focus returns to the real issues, you'll be worse off than when you started.

4) Let's Rewrite History

Here's a frequent scenario I've seen played out. Joel is a high-level leader with the company. He's edified by both the team and the company, serves on committees or councils, and is featured prominently at events and online broadcasts. Then Joel decides to leave and join another company. Suddenly the story turns to, "Well, we didn't really want to say anything, but Joel is actually a womanizing bank robber who was caught stealing money from the Pope."

Trying to demonize and discredit someone after the fact always backfires on you. Because team members rightfully think, "If he really was such an evil person, why were they edifying him when it was convenient for them?"

5) Let's Spin This as a Victory

The craziest example of this I've seen was a company under severe legal attack. The CEO/founder was being sued by his siblings as well as being charged by the government for tax evasion. The siblings won a $10 million judgment and the government sent the CEO to prison. What was the official company position? These were great victories.

They sent out announcements that because the judgment was "only" $10 million, such a lenient award showed that the court supported their position. And they told leaders that since this prison housed only nonviolent, white-collar offenders, the severity of the crime was akin to getting a speeding ticket. During the CEO's incarceration, they referred to him as being at "camp."

Almost unbelievably, this company still survives today. But it is a textbook example of a flatline company. The people who drank the Kool-Aid hang on, but the only way to increase sales is by opening additional countries, because no one takes the company or its field leadership seriously in the existing markets. Nobody wants to join a flatline company.

Often these five reactions are based on a well-meaning desire to protect a team from anything negative ever happening to them. And while this goal is noble, it's not realistic. The truth is, bad things are eventually going to happen to everyone, including your team.

The mark of a positive, empowering leader isn't that you will prevent anything bad from happening—because that simply isn't possible—but rather that you will show (lead) the team how to come out on the other side still standing.

LEAD THROUGH THE BAD TO THE OTHER SIDE

So how do you do that? We're going to explore that throughout the rest of this book. But let's set the foundation here. Let's revisit the definition of a leader I gave you in the introduction:

Inspiring people to become the highest possible version of themselves—and building the environment that facilitates this process. Here's what that looks like in practical application:

You use your power to make those who follow you more powerful.

There are lots of parental analogies we can use here, but the best one is that of "helicopter parents." Just as these parents harm their children by hovering over them constantly, trying to protect them, you can create the same result with your team. You need to protect your kids from pedophiles and kidnappers, but you have to allow them to skin their knees and fall off their bikes. The omnipotent, charismatic, dynamic leader who for all practical purposes runs a benevolent cult ultimately weakens his people and destroys the team. They suck all of the oxygen out of the room.

We can take my definition of strong leadership above and break it down into two components. The first part is about inspiring team members to become the highest possible version of themselves. To do that begins with leading yourself. You have to be the example, the person modeling the behavior, and most importantly, the one going after your own dreams.

There are legions of negative people who will doubt you, ridicule you, and even try to sabotage you. If you're not willing to fight for your dreams, the haters win. Your team needs to see you winning this fight yourself in order for them even to have a shot.

The ironic thing about inspiring leadership is that it doesn't come from simply being positive and recognizing good results. To actually inspire others, you must challenge them in some way. People look to leaders because they want someone who dares them to have a higher vision, raise their eyes above the horizon, and strive to accomplish more, whether for themselves or a noble purpose.

The best way to do that is always by modeling the behavior. Barking orders at people certainly isn't going to work. We place way too much emphasis on control in our profession. Because we're dealing with an all-volunteer army, control doesn't actually work very well. When you operate in control mode, you're really offering people only two options: Comply or Defy. And since most people hate being told what to do, a lot choose the latter option.

Simply becoming the world's best trainer and presenting the world's finest training won't succeed either. (Especially if you're not actually doing what you teach yourself.) Your team will draw the biggest cues from watching the actions and behaviors they see from you. So be the example showing them the path to follow.

The second part of strong leadership is building the environment that facilitates your people's process of becoming their highest version of themselves. This is an important responsibility of all top leaders in Leveraged Sales. You do this through the system, training, and tools. It's also vital that there be a defined leadership track to follow.

Your people need to know what the pathway for becoming a leader with the team looks like. If you're a new recruit in the army and your dream is to become a general, you have an idea of what all the ranks leading up to that rank are and the responsibilities of each one. Your people need to know what ranks, behaviors, and team activities put them on the path of becoming a leader with the team. (This will become much clearer to you in later chapters.)

Once you are working well in these two areas—inspiring people to become better and creating an environment that facilitates that—you have the two fundamental elements for developing a strong infrastructure of leadership throughout your team. This will allow you to develop strong growth and true duplication.

Now that you know what the role of a positive, empowering leader looks like, let's explore the most important step you will take towards that end—accepting the sacred responsibility that comes along with sponsoring others.

CHAPTER 2

The Sacred Responsibility of Sponsoring

For decades I've been regaling convention audiences with my story of sponsoring my roommate into the first five companies I joined. (In fact, the story is so funny it's been stolen by one CEO, two authors, and five other speakers. That I know of.) He joined each time because I agreed to pay for his distributor kit and activation order, for which he promised to repay me from all the money we were both going to be raking in. And in each of those attempts, he was the *only* person I sponsored!

That system works well to sign up your first recruit quickly but doesn't work out so well over the long haul. After I reached the point where I couldn't even convince my roommate to join if I paid for everything, it became apparent I would need to improve my recruiting approach.

Mentally I created a pretty simple equation in my mind. It basically went something like this:

- I was broke and I hated being broke.
- Most of the people I knew were also broke.
- The people in Leveraged Sales made money, earned bonus cars, and went on fancy trips. A lot

of them appeared to be rich (and certainly were rich by my standards).

- I wanted to be rich.
- If I could sign up enough people, I would get rich.
- If the people I signed up also signed up enough people, they could get rich too.

That was my basic recruiting presentation. Eventually I got good enough at that pitch to attract and sponsor people who actually paid for their own distributor kit and activation order. I felt assured that I was well on my way to success, because I had conquered the most difficult element of the business: recruiting. I did my part by signing up at least five people and then waited for them to make me rich. (Because I had seen the presentation that said those five would bring in 25, then those 25 would bring in 125, and so on.) It was all I could do to restrain myself from putting down the deposit to order my Ferrari.

Shockingly, I noticed that my five people didn't seem to be pulling their weight. I checked in with them frequently, reminding them that I needed to be rich and they weren't doing their part. You've probably deduced how well that played out.

FEELING FRUSTRATED, I RESOLVED TO BECOME A RECRUITING MACHINE

I would sponsor so many people, there would be no way that duplication could *not* happen. (Or so I thought.) I started doing meetings five nights a week in the back room of a local restaurant. The skill level (and pressure tactics) of my presenting moved upwards and sponsor-ships increased to 30 people in a month. Those 30 people would naturally increase to at least 150 the following month, right?

The actual number was a net loss of 27.

I decided that those 30 people were obviously too stupid, ignorant, and lazy, and I needed to replace them with 30 new people. Which I did...

Surprisingly, I got pretty much the same result. Again and again, the people I sponsored were too stupid, igno-rant, and lazy. Finally, I had no option but to once again seriously examine the way I was attempting to build. It turns out, the problem wasn't my recruits. The problem was me.

I came to understand that the method I was using to bring people into the business could not be duplicated by most of those people.

REEXAMINING MY PROCESS

And that was a frustrating and disappointing revelation. But it transformed my career. That introspection led me to creating what became the duplicable system that made me successful. How to create that system is not the subject here. (If you're not familiar with it, you can find it detailed in my last book, *Direct Selling Success*.) But here was the other vital breakthrough I discovered in this process:

You have a sacred responsibility to those you sponsor. By bringing them into the business, you are committing to be a partner for their success, not just your own.

This doesn't mean you should make them codepend-ent or do their work for them. It doesn't mean you should be stacking people under them in the structure to prop them up or qualify them at a higher rank. But it does mean that just like having a child or adopting a pet, there are going to be changes needed in your routine, schedule, and priorities. Every time you enroll a new team member, you are implicitly agreeing to play a part in their development.

When I changed my perspective from believ-ing that the reason for sponsoring someone was so they could make me rich to a belief that I should be recruiting people only if I were committed to being a partner for their success, that really changed the game for me. And it will for you.

LEADING YOURSELF

Leadership in Leveraged Sales begins with leading your-self. And the building block of that personal leadership is how you conduct yourself with the people you personally enroll into the business.

It's trendy to talk about servant leadership, but I fear that concept has been misconstrued deeply. Servant leadership has come to mean sacrifice and altruism, but that is not the real concept of this kind of leadership. True leaders understand the virtue of a certain kind of selfishness. Let me explain.

Your First Responsibility as a Leader Is to Become Successful

Not because you're supposed to be selfish, but because discovering the correct path, becoming successful yourself, and then modeling that behavior is the most helpful—and selfless—way to lead your team. You can't show anyone how to become a specific rank in the compensation plan unless you have attained that rank yourself.

Let's revisit the wise words of the legendary Zig Ziglar: "You will get all you want in life...if you just help enough other people get what they want." No arguments from me. But in terms of *practical application*, what that means in our business is that you blaze the trail first. It's well meaning to think you should help your team become successful first, but that's not how it actually works.

You learned in my earlier definition of leadership that the first element is inspiring people to become the highest possible version of themselves. That isn't accomplished by your remaining static and lecturing your team on why they should grow. If you want to actually inspire people, you do so by modeling the path they will need to follow. Approach your responsibility with the mindset of pursuing your own success, while reaching down a helping hand to your personal enrollees and bringing them along the journey with you.

Once you're doing this, you're meeting the first requirement, inspiring others to become the highest possible version of themselves. But what about part two—enabling an environment that facilitates the process? Let's unpack what that looks like.

BUILD THE FOUNDATION

A huge part of this involves having the right infrastructure in place: training procedures for team members, tools that help them develop skillsets, events for promoting the business to candidates, and a delineated "ladder of escalation" that candidates are brought through. This infrastructure helps the team handle the mechanics of building the business. I spent a great deal of ink explaining that in *Direct Selling Success*, so I won't repeat that info here. The focus of this field manual is to dissect and explain your leadership responsibilities in this process.

As you've probably deduced, one of your foremost concerns must always be the duplicability of what you practice and teach. This requires a deft touch and some intellectual nuance. There are many potential problem situations along the way.

Time Expectations

For example, once you're a successful leader, you could easily be working 30 to 50 hours a week running your business. But the business practices you teach your new enrollees to follow must be able to be accomplished in 10 to 15 hours a week, maximum. (Because most people will be entering the business part-time, along with working their existing job and practicing their other family and societal obligations.) Because we work from home, our business has very little separation between work life and personal life, and it can easily become all consuming. Let's explore an interesting way you could set off a tripwire that harms your people, when you're simply trying to help them and be friendly: socializing with them.

You might think it would be a great idea to have a regular social event for your local team. It could be something as innocuous as playing laser tag or putting together a bowling league. This can actually be harmful.

Here's why: The new people in your group will be trying to finesse the adjustment from their normal schedule to finding 10 to 15 hours a week to work their new business. For a lot of people, this will create stress in other areas, often their family life. Their spouse might see the new business as unwanted competition for the team member's already scarce free time. If the new team member adds another evening a week for social time with your group, this could be the tipping point that moves the spouse from guarded support or skepticism to outright opposition. You can end up losing team members over this.

Financial Realities

Often this creates financial stress as well. If you're a successful mid-level distributor in the business, spending $20 for lunch or $35 on a social event probably means nothing to you. But to someone who is starting out in a tight financial situation and investing in their new business, even relatively minor expenditures like these can become quite stressful. And as your business (and income) grows, the amount of stress you create for your team can become more pronounced. After you're successful, you might be eating at restaurants where dinner is $500 a person or staying in hotel suites costing $2,000 a night. Trying to keep up with you could then produce a serious threat to their family budget.

You may find that instead of your people getting "fired up" about the rewards of success, they are demoralized because they aren't traveling in those kinds of circles yet and are fearful about their ability to get there.

Social Connections

Certainly, social connection is a huge part of our business. For that reason, I recommend you build parties or social connection into your regular team training events. For example, as we design the agenda for our two- or three-day major events, we usually make Saturday night a party night. We have a different theme each time (disco party, '80s night, talent show, superhero costumes, etc.).

Another example is the practice of giving gifts during the holiday season. My recommendation is you set the culture in your team that could include a team-wide celebration and well wishes, but no exchange of gifts. This might appear counterintuitive to you, as it does to many people. Leaders love the idea of giving gifts of business or personal development items, as doing so seems inspirational and congruent with the philosophy of growth in the business. But once again, there could be stress points.

Someone just working their way up through the comp plan could be at a level where they have 80 or 100 members on their team and are reinvesting all they earn back into the business (buying recruiting tools, building long-distance lines, etc.). If they want to buy gifts for everyone, it could require going into debt, which would not be prudent.

There are people I respect who have a culture of gift giving, considering this integral to relationship building, showing appreciation, and creating loyalty. They have systemized the process, including team guidelines on who you give a gift to and how much to spend. If you're going to have a culture of gift giving, be sure and follow their example.

As you can see, some practices look benign on the surface but end up backfiring in the important area of duplicability. Begin by leading yourself, then filter everything through the lens of how it will affect the people many levels below you. Once you've made this commitment to the success of those you sponsor and worked to ensure that the infrastructure and team practices promote duplicability, you have to do something unusual in business (and even relationships) today...

CARE ENOUGH ABOUT YOUR PEOPLE TO BE A TRUTH TELLER

If you read my last book, you know I make two promises to everyone I enroll:

1. I will never knowingly lie to them.
2. I will never knowingly tell them something that is not in the best interests of their business.

But being a truth teller goes much further. It means you respect people enough that you don't pander to them or just tell them what they want to hear. Nothing is more harmful to a person's growth and development than having coaches or mentors who only compliment and indulge them with "happy talk" and don't keep their guidance grounded in reality. Most of us have surrounded ourselves with people who give us permission to stay the same. We all need people in our lives who love and respect us for who we are—yet also challenge us to become better versions of ourselves.

Let me share a story from early in my career about the first time I met some people high up in my sponsorship line, a couple who were one of the top-earning distribu-torships in the world. They told me something that dev-astated me—and ultimately created one of the biggest breakthroughs in my life.

That couple was Spencer and Shivani Poch. They lived in Sacramento, with a team that spanned all around the country. I was in Miami, hundreds of levels down in their organization. They had heard about a training I was conducting for my team and asked if I would be willing to come to California and present it to their group there. Of course, this was the highest honor they could bestow upon me, elevating and edifying me on their stage. I eagerly jumped at the opportunity.

The evening before the event, they graciously took me out for dinner, so we could get to know each other. I was starstruck just spending time with them, eager to impress them with my work ethic, tenacity, and desire to become successful. I did what I always did in those days: regale them with story after story of the trauma, drama, and victimhood in my life.

I explained what a loser my own sponsor was and how much harder I had to work because of him. I spoke about the guy who had his credit card declined for his order on the last day of the month, which meant he didn't qualify for a rank, which in turn made me unqualified for my rank and cost me a lot of commissions. (There was no Internet then. You didn't know your actual sales and rank until two weeks later, when the checks were issued.) I complained about all the lazy ignorant people in my team, my health challenges, my dysfunctional relation-ships, and all of the other unfair things the universe was assaulting me with at that point in my life.

Looking back on that dinner now, I can recognize my whining for what it truly was: working my fulltime job as a professional victim. This whole story was an almost prerecorded "data dump" I did anytime I talked about myself. It was my desperate subconscious attempt to feel worthy, just an innocent victim fighting the forces of evil. I had zero awareness of this at the time of our dinner in California.

I thought I was just explaining why all of the bad things that happened to me weren't my fault, that I was simply a very unlucky person the universe was conspiring against. I was quite sure Spence and Shivani were duly impressed with my strength and resilience. Until we were getting into the car after the dinner.

Just before we climbed into the car, Spence looked at me and asked quietly, "Randy, have you given any thought to what you might be doing to attract all of these bad things in your life?"

Time Stood Still

I was perplexed. Which quickly escalated to apoplectic. My mind began racing... Did he not hear everything I had just told him? Was he not listening? Was he just a cold-hearted sonofabitch?

I'm not sure what I mumbled back, but I'm sure it showed I wasn't buying into his woo-woo, New-Age thinking. I did the training the next day and returned home. But that question had me grinding my molars for the next few weeks. My thoughts swirled, collided, detonated, and ultimately left me dazed. Wasn't I simply an innocent victim? Could I really be somehow attracting those calamities into my life? Spencer's question forced me into deep introspection. This finally led to my asking myself the most important question I have ever asked myself. As I reflected on my many health challenges, business failures, and dysfunctional relationships, I asked:

Was there one person who was always at the scene of the crime?

I didn't like the answer I got. But that answer was what liberated me from lack and limitation. It meant taking personal responsibility, and instead of thinking of myself as a recipient in my life, seeing myself as a co-creator. I realized that I had lived in a victimhood mindset my entire existence up until that moment of clarity. And that if I wanted things to change, *I* would have to change.

I stopped looking at external, outside factors, and began to think about the internal, inside ones.

Now, decades later, I can still look back to that simple question Spence had asked me and recognize it as a seminal moment in my life, one that started my transformation and turned things around for me. And that was all because instead of pandering to me, he cared enough about me to be brutally honest—to be a truth teller. And there is no greater gift you can give the people on your team, especially the ones you enroll personally. Be that truth teller.

LOOK INWARD

Another vital part of your responsibility as a truth teller is to be honest with yourself as well. People need leaders who are rational, realistic, and cognizant of their own strengths and weaknesses. My breakthrough came when I looked at my situation: numerous health challenges, business failures, and negative, dysfunctional relationships. I certainly met the first of the criteria from von Mises that we discussed in Chapter 1: I was dissatisfied.

Changing your behavior in an area requires doing the introspection to recognize that you are dissatisfied with your current situation, then creating a compelling vision of something better. You need a vision magnetic enough to pull you toward it. Then it gets harder.

MAKE YOUR OWN PATH

Instead of waiting around for some inspirational leader to create a way for you to become prosperous, you have to figure it out for yourself. You have to create the path that you're confident will get you there. (Because if you don't see that path, you'll never get out of inertia mode.) Now you're probably wondering about your sponsor, and whether this isn't their job. Technically it is. But you can't count on that. If you want to be one of the best in our business, you must learn self-reliance.

Perhaps the most trying part of all this is the requirement that you leave behind victim mode and accept responsibility for manifesting your own destiny. That means you can't get away with excuses. And you can't blame your lack of success upon your sponsor, the company, or the profession. You have to accept responsibility for your own success—or lack of it.

This is not to say that you won't encounter legitimate obstacles to manifesting that success. You certainly will. But so will everyone else. You can be a victim or a victor, but you can't be both. You either choose to accept excuses and relegate yourself to victimhood or you commit to overcoming those obstacles and becoming a victor.

You don't become successful because you have no challenges. You become successful because you choose to overcome your challenges. You choose to do the difficult work of effort, growth, and self-development.

It is only after you accept and implement this reality that you can become the kind of inspiring sponsor to your personal enrollees, and by extension, a model of leadership for the team. Which is what we will explore next.

CHAPTER 3

How You Become a Model Leader

For my first five years in the business, I struggled financially and couldn't get anyone to follow me. Later I earned over a million dollars annually in commissions and had followers all over the world. What was the big difference?

WHO I HAD BECOME

That's the funny thing about leadership. Before people follow you, they kinda sorta expect you to possess a certain character, people skills, and, you know, leadership ability.

I'm one of the feel-good, rags-to-riches success stories. The riches are the fun side of the story. The other side is the kind of person I was during the "rags" phase.

I didn't join the business to save the world, finance orphanages, or fund a cure for cancer. I wanted a Ferrari, a movie-star-level mansion, and enough bling-bling hanging around my neck that I needed help getting up from the sofa. I was the definition of cupidity and joined because I hated being poor and was desperate to become rich.

And desperate people do desperate things. Unfortunately, my desperation carried through in my prospecting approaches, scaring away almost anyone with a good sense of judging people. And the few people who did join my team soon came to resent my constantly goading them to do more, aka make me more money. I was not a leader or anything approaching one. But there was one saving grace of this business that rescued me from certain failure. That saving grace was this fact:

In Leveraged Sales, personal development is baked into the cake of the business model, and everyone who enters the profession grows as a person—or self-selects to leave.

Self-Development

If you know what's good for you, you will embrace this reality with every cell in your body. Because it can be the saving grace for you as well. I've never seen another business where self-development is such an integral part of the career path. To become the kind of leader we're talking about in this field manual, you'll want to practice self-development religiously and create a culture where your team does the same.

You need to practice this self-development for two reasons: First, to become proficient at new skillsets. And second, to develop into a better person and leader—the highest possible version of yourself.

Because of the Internet, mobile apps, and podcasts, we're living in the golden age for enlightenment. It's never been easier to create a customized learning program for your personal growth and career advancement.

SKILLSETS FOR SUCCESS

If you've followed my earlier work, you already know there are four basic skillsets you must become proficient at in the early stage of your career:

- Meeting people
- Working a candidate list
- Inviting
- Follow-up

Those are the skillsets everyone needs to master as quickly as possible, and the ones to teach in your new member orientation. (I covered these extensively in *Direct Selling Success*, so I won't repeat that information here.) When you move into the leadership ranks, you will need more advanced skills. I'm recommending that you integrate the following topics of study into the "core curriculum" of your self-development program. **Note:** These skills are not required for beginners and I'm not recommending you teach them to new people. Doing so will slow your growth and hamper duplication. These are the skills required to become a DEFCON 1 leader.

They are:

- Public speaking and presenting
- Team building
- Conflict resolution
- Leadership strategies

The reasons for some of these skills are self-apparent; others are not as evident. Let's briefly go through why they're required and what they can do for you and your team.

Public Speaking and Presenting

When you become skillful at public speaking, you can inspire your team, teach them new skills, build their belief, *and* compel qualified candidates to become customers and team members. People in Leveraged Sales don't place enough emphasis on the skillset of presenting to large audiences (both online and offline). Because when you become a remarkable platform presenter, your business begins to grow exponentially. The two are intertwined.

Even when doing in-home presentations, the better you are at presenting, the more successful you will become. And becoming a compelling, charismatic speaker will make a *huge* difference once you are on the platform at a hotel or any other large venues for opportunity presentations (including online live streams). It should go without saying, but won't, that *you also need to be captivating when you're conducting training seminars and workshops for your team.*

It's just a fact: the most successful people in any company are usually the best speakers. There is a link between being a good platform speaker and being a strong trainer. When you have good platform skills, you lead, inspire, and communicate better. Your team is better trained, and you will experience stronger duplication down the ranks.

The greatest moment in any speech is when someone in the audience reacts to the speaker with this thought: "Wow, you too? I thought I was the only one in the world with that issue. I'm so relieved to learn that there is hope for me." Whether it's a candidate in an opportunity presentation or a team member in a training event—this is the moment when everything "clicks," and behavior is changed for the better. When you become a rock star presenter, you create these magic moments over and over again. And this is the level of skill you need to develop.

Team Building

Team-building skills are beneficial for the obvious reasons. The better you get at these, the larger your group will grow. You'll also become much more productive as you learn how to work multiple lines at the same time to produce synergistic results. A great spinoff benefit is that your team develops a strong identity, providing the members with a sense of belonging that improves morale and retention. Your team-building skills come into play in a plethora of areas. Some examples are communicating with the team, setting training agendas, running events, and providing recognition. This material was also covered extensively in *Direct Selling Success*, so I won't repeat here.

Set the Pace.

Another fundamental element of leadership is setting the pace for the team. Every organization has a culture established by the leader. Some leaders are so demanding and operate at such a furious pace they end up leaving talented, motivated people behind. Other leaders pander to the lowest common denominator. This approach frustrates the high achievers and will ultimately drive them away. The best approach is where you keep the team slightly breathless to keep up. They can see the train is leaving the station, and they're breathing a little quicker to catch up and jump on before the door closes. People respond best to leaders who challenge them to become more. Be that leader.

Conflict Resolution

Now we get to the messy stuff. Conflict resolution.

This is why you get the big bucks. Because this is the thorniest part of leading a cohesive team, which is vital for duplication. From a scientific standpoint, cohesion attraction is the action or property of like molecules sticking together, being mutually attractive. But you can take one cursory look at your leadership team and probably deduce that they aren't mutually attractive. You undoubtedly have different generations, ethnicities, nationalities, genders, political ideologies, and dozens of other things. And then we have to throw in other factors like egos, hurt feelings, status signaling, jealousy, and entitlement.

The stark reality of leading a large team is that only about 40 percent of your time will be devoted to managing functions, setting training agendas, conducting events, leading the team, and actual day-to-day business building. As a top leader, you will be spending 60 percent of your time and mental bandwidth on conflict resolution. Really. Let's talk about how you can do this successfully and effectively.

Here's the type of issues that will take up the bulk of your time, energy, and brainpower for the rest of your career:

Geoffrey sponsors Sabastian. Geoffrey also sponsored Rebecca, who is a personal trainer to both of them, and now Sabastian feels that his sponsor has "stolen" his best prospect.

Jim and José are crossline, but they became friends. When Jim opened a gym, he got José to invest in it. Now the gym has gone out of business and José wants you to get his investment back.

Lisa sponsors Luis and Henry and places one on each side of her structure. Then she sponsors Dan and places him under Luis. Henry is despondent and feels he's been cheated because you didn't place anyone under him.

Richard sponsors Erik and quickly places another five people down that line. Next month Erik is upset because he doesn't get any more spillover.

And these issues aren't only from your beginning team members. Wait until you see what your top leaders have in store for you.

Benjamin is upset because he wasn't included on the new company recruiting video. Paul isn't speaking to you because you gave Alejandra 10 minutes more stage time than he got. Sasha posted a scathing political rant on Facebook and now 20 people on his team want to quit.

You will be assaulted almost daily with issues that you think are trivial, insignificant, or meaningless. But to the people bringing them to you, these are the most monumental issues facing humankind. It's going to be your job to sort through the conflicts, kill the distractions, and get people back to work.

I wish there were a scientific formula and explainable process for conflict resolution similar to the way we can detail how a caterpillar becomes a butterfly or how to farm soybeans. Unfortunately, there isn't. Like I said, this is the messy part. But I will share everything I have learned in terms of resolving conflicts with the best possible outcomes. Let's start with a foundational principle.

Confront Issues and Comfort People.

Too many people think that if issues are ignored, they are going to miraculously disappear or somehow resolve themselves. Not likely. If someone feels slighted, believes they have been treated unfairly, or thinks that they are being disrespected, that issue is quite real to them and needs to be dealt with. And sometimes the solution they seek is simply not possible or realistic. Do your best to see if the issue can be resolved to their satisfaction. If it can't, at least you have demonstrated your concern for them.

Get the Parties Together.

You're going to have lots of people who want to corner you alone and plead their case against someone else. Don't allow that to happen; get the parties together. Someone may call you and say something like this:

> Them: "I have a big problem with Daniel. Don't tell him I called you, but—"
>
> You: "Sorry to interrupt. If you have a problem with Daniel, we need to get him on the call right now. Hang on while I see if he's available."
>
> Them: "Wait, I don't want him to know that I'm the one who complained."
>
> You: "Sorry, I never talk about someone else when they're not present. If we really want to solve this problem, we are going to have to handle

this like adults. We need to get the three of us on the phone together and discuss the issues openly."

You have to be the grownup in the room. When you handle situations in that way, your team understands that you don't play games or deal in gossip. Your deliberate action kills the organizational politics, thus creating an environment where issues can be resolved. This also ensures that toxic people who are simply addicted to drama will recognize that they can't play that game in your team and they'll move on to somewhere else.

Work to Stay Away from Personal Attacks and Focus on the Issues Involved.

People default to drama and love to be distracted from the work at hand. Let's suppose that Mohammed has an issue with something Hunter did; maybe Hunter said something in a training that Mohammed believes is incorrect. You solve that issue and the next thing you know Mohammed is digressing into distractions because he thinks Hunter has a screechy voice, needs a haircut, or isn't intelligent enough. You're going to have to work to keep swatting away the distractions and restore the focus on solving the original issue and getting people back to work.

Keep Politics and Favoritism Out. Concentrate on Just and Fair Outcomes.

Nothing produces more conflict than playing favorites and allowing politics to influence decisions. To have a team working cohesively, you must practice a meritocracy.

The "perks" of team leadership (things like stage time, being featured in marketing materials, and recognition at events) should always be allocated on the merits of the results produced. If you favor someone who isn't achieving success—just because they are your personal enrollee—over someone who is a strong producer in the field, you're guaranteeing yourself a lot of conflict. If you run your team as a true meritocracy you will have a lot more harmony (and a lot less drama), so you'll be able to concentrate on growing sales instead of constantly putting out fires.

Always Come Down on the Side of Integrity.

Sad to say, but an overwhelming majority of the issues you will have to deal with involve dishonest behavior. Some of the frequent complaints involve people trying to steal prospects from other distributors, distributors trying to switch lines using different ID numbers, manipulating orders or volume to qualify at ranks, creating fake distributorships to game the compensation plan, and front-loading new distributors with excess inventory.

You must always make your decisions to support the right and honest outcomes, even when (especially when) the outcome does not benefit you in the way you would like. Let me give you two powerful examples of my having to make a difficult decision, the great pain it caused, but how eventually the outcomes proved to be the best I could have hoped for.

About 10 years ago, I had a vibrant team developing in Germany. It was led by a personal enrollee I had met on a trip to Europe. Volume was growing, rank advancements were occurring on a regular basis, and the group there was contributing nicely to my own bonus check. I started hearing some murmuring and backhanded comments about my enrollee, but no one would be a big kid and tell me anything specific. At first I played them off as the normal grumblings of people who were afraid of hard work. But the volume intensified, and I was finally able to get one of the mid-level leaders there whom I respected to open up to me. He informed me that my enrollee required all the people he enrolled to supply him with their back office login to the website.

On the last night of every pay period, my enrollee would go into his people's accounts and create orders (which were charged to them) to ensure that certain people achieved certain ranks—which also meant that *he* would qualify for the highest possible bonus. He had quietly been getting away with this for months. The problem was coming to a head only now, because he was actually deleting enrollments his team made and then reentering them—assigning the sponsorship to himself.

When I confronted my guy with these accusations, he immediately admitted to doing them. In the past, he had worked in another company where this was standard leadership behavior, so he understood this to be an acceptable practice and acted in the same way. This behavior was not only unethical and dishonest, it actually jeopardized the entire company. Practices like this can get you closed down by the regulators.

I immediately took the results of my investigation to the corporate executive team. They were shocked—but also mindful of the volume the German group was generating. They wanted to just warn the distributor responsible and suspend him for one month. I demanded that he be terminated, even though I expected to take a serious income hit. The behavior was too far over the line of integrity to warrant anything less. Because I was so adamant, the company complied.

What happened next was surprising and delightful. Instead of the volume tanking, it actually went up. The people in the field saw that not only did I have their backs, I demonstrated that integrity and doing the right thing was an essential component of the team culture.

A few years later, another case arose, one with even greater potential downside risks. I was the number one income earner in my company, with one of my personal enrollees holding the number two spot. Obviously, his group made up a large part of my own. He was definitely a grinder, worked very deep in depth, and had given away personal enrollments to others, helping them achieve ranks sooner. My involvement with this group was less, because they had an alpha leader, were far away, and spoke a different language. Pretty much all my interaction with the group went through my guy.

Unfortunately, he had a strong ego and wanted to be feted and lionized by his people. Not everyone was willing to do that. He had a couple of leaders who he believed didn't acknowledge the role he played in their success. He started demeaning them publicly on social media. I tried to shut that down, but he persisted, and in fact, increased his attacks. The company got involved and warned him that his actions violated the Policies and Procedures (P&Ps) and continuing those actions would get him terminated.

The company execs and I did some Skype calls with him, trying to deescalate the situation. My guy felt that we were meddling with his business and once again escalated his public campaign against his own people. I woke up one morning to discover he had actually posted photos of people's back office, incomes, and government ID numbers on Facebook. Now he was threatening the golden goose. I called the company president and asked for him to be immediately terminated, which he was.

That leader was my friend. I probably earned at least half a million dollars a year annually from that line. The last thing I wanted to do was see him terminated. But my responsibility as a leader—and your responsibility as a leader—is to protect your team. And that means the company as well. If the company ain't around, ain't gonna be nobody getting bonus checks.

There are cases where the death penalty (immediate termination) is required. Do this swiftly and publicly, so people understand what is and isn't accepted in your culture. And if the regulators do come after your company, this strong, definitive action demonstrates that the company polices their own team and does not sanction or condone any illegal behavior. As a leader, you should not only support your company in this way, but you may have to be the one who insists on that decision. Not all company owners and execs will have the courage to do the right thing. They hate to lose potential sales as much as the field does. But you've got to stand for integrity above all else. When you have people who act illegally, steal recruits, or flout the P&Ps, you need to self-police, not wait and hope someone else does it. Good leadership requires this.

I'm happy to tell you that in the example above, my team there rebounded and eventually started growing again. Once again, the team members in the group understood that we cared for them, stood for integrity, and would always do the right thing. Nothing builds a greater loyalty (or stronger business) than this.

Leadership Strategies

If you're wondering when we are going to get to the "leadership strategies" part of leadership skills, we already have. I punked you a little by implying that leadership strategies are a separate skillset category. Truth is, there aren't actually many skills or behaviors designed to effectively lead for the sake of leadership. You lead by how you organize, communicate, handle conflict resolution, conduct yourself, demonstrate integrity, and just generally model leadership behaviors. You become a great leader not because you successfully pass the "Leadership 101 test" or become proficient in advanced leadership strategies. You become a great leader by responding the right way in all of the areas we've just discussed.

You model the behavior that will allow people to be successful and create an environment where they are inspired to model you.

Great leaders don't just solve problems and make sure the trains run on time. Perhaps the most important element of leadership is creating a positive vision for your team. It's vital that you raise people's eyes above the horizon, so they focus on a bigger and bolder future for all. Because that greater vision is the superglue that keeps people firmly attached to the team when there are challenges and obstacles along the way. Model leaders set the vision and then show the pathway to that vision through hard work, professionalism, and integrity.

You might be reading all this and thinking that the skills required for leading your team require that you become a psychologist. (I have felt that way on more occasions than I care to recount.) Fortunately, you won't need to get that Ph.D. degree in psychology. The real breakthrough in this area comes from self-awareness and living in congruence with principles. As you begin to watch yourself, and understand the consequences of your actions upon others, you will develop clear and strong insights on the motivations and behaviors of this mysterious species we call human.

A situation you will encounter far too often in our profession is the 20-year veterans who, instead of having 20 years of compounded experience, have one year of experience, 20 times. They know only the same solutions to fall back on and rely on situational templates: "This is the way you handle alcoholics, this other way is how you work with single parents, this is the way you deal with sidelines, this is how you handle enrollees, this is how you interact with the sponsorship line above you," and so on.

But that isn't what leadership is about.

Leadership is dealing with each unique person in a way that helps them unlock the issues for them. What I seek to do with this manual is teach you how to become a wise leader—one who can then use wisdom, empathy, and discernment to create solutions based on strong character and by following a set of principles.

Leadership isn't about the actions you take but the actual person you become. Once you've become the right person, you never have to ask questions like "What would Jesus do?" Because the right course of action will always be what you would do—because of who you have become.

Culture is one of the platforms you can employ to lead your team to greatness. And that's what we will explore next.

CHAPTER 4

Unleashing Your Secret Weapon: Culture

Culture truly is the secret weapon of every great team leader who creates solid duplication and continued growth. As we discussed in the last chapter, it's foolish to try and prepare a course of action for every possible scenario a team member may face in their recruiting and day-to-day operation of their business. If you could even create such a manual, it would be a 50,000-page binder and would make the business completely unduplicable.

Culture is the answer. It's your secret weapon for productivity, duplication, and success.

Becoming a positive empowering leader consists of three foundational steps:

1. Create the vision.
2. Build the community.
3. Set the culture.

Don't make yourself the star or you'll suck all of the oxygen from the room. Make the team and team culture the star, because that is what maintains the self-preservation of the organization. Culture sets the tone for the team, prepares your people for what's ahead, and lets them know exactly what kind of organization they are a part of. Most importantly, it gives them principles and values to guide them through difficult decisions.

Recruiting contests, pop culture trends, and hot social media platforms are ephemeral. Their only constant is change, and you'll be hard-pressed to keep your team trained on how to react to the ever-moving target. When you set culture, however, you're creating principles that transcend the temporary and work effectively over the course of time.

But that doesn't mean you set culture and you're done.

It doesn't work that way. Your culture will evolve over time. Especially as you face challenges and crises, and especially when you make mistakes. You learn and grow from them and your culture adapts accordingly. The most important thing I can ever teach you about culture is this: Team culture doesn't exist apart from the actual team.

YOUR TEAM DOESN'T *HAVE* A CULTURE. IT *IS* A CULTURE.

It's difficult to get 50,000 people in a team to behave appropriately. But if the right culture is in place, it becomes a lot more possible and probable. Culture is what transforms a bunch of unrelated people with individual goals, dreams, and objectives into a cohesive team on a mission. Culture isn't really a set of beliefs, but a construct of how the team handles various situations. Your culture telegraphs to the outside world who you really are. And most importantly, what it will mean to work with you.

Does your team care about people's families or laser focus on how to make more money? Do your people hug or bow or shake hands? Is your team building a large customer base or concentrating only on recruiting recruiters? Do you meet at the Four Seasons or the Holiday Inn?

Let's look at some of the most important areas in which culture is created – and the kind of culture that is best for each. If you've followed my work over the years, you'll see that my thinking on this has evolved to reflect changes in society, business, and technology.

INTEGRITY

One area of my thinking that has not changed is the necessity of creating a culture of integrity for your team. There are no shortcuts or substitutions for doing the right thing. Having a good reputation is one of the most valuable assets you'll ever have to build a business. (And just as valuable in many other areas of your life.) If you squander it for a quick recruiting or income increase, you'll pay a negative price the rest of your career.

Every person starts a new group of their own, even though they are a part of a larger team. So even though you are a part of your sponsor's group, and the group above them, your organization's culture still begins with you. Make sure you're the "firewall" that prevents anything illegal, immoral, or unethical from reaching below you.

ETHOS

By ethos culture, I mean the distinguishing spirit and vibe of your team. Some teams have all the guys in suits and ties and the gals in pants suits. Other teams dress business casual. Some have presentations that are very corporate-like and business-only in tone, while others have fun, light-hearted presentations that resemble a social get-together more than a business meeting.

Perhaps the most impactful part of your ethos is the vision you create. In my last book I advised you to build a dream bigger than your team. It's important that you articulate a bold, valiant, and compelling outcome that speaks to the aspirations of your people. Nothing else in our lives provides such a tremendous feeling of satisfaction and belonging as being intrinsically connected to a force, project, or movement for good. Something larger than ourselves.

Your team will chase after the free trips, bonus cars, and other rewards. But if you can pair that pursuit of profit with a plan for higher good, they'll certainly become yet more energized. Sometimes this is moving toward a positive result, such as building an orphanage or funding a freshwater well for a remote village. Other times it may be fighting a common foe that your product line addresses (Big Pharma or insurance companies that rip off people, for example). Whichever way you go, make it bold, daring, and aspirational. *People love to be a part of something bigger than themselves and you'll end up doing more by doing good.*

Another huge determinant to your ethos will be how you balance customer building with recruiting.

For far too many years, the ethos of network marketing and MLM was way too over-indexed on sign-ups and recruiting. If we lose sight of the foundation of product sales to ultimate consumers, everything falls apart. A big part of the reason I am promoting the concept of Leveraged Sales so evangelically is because it keeps equal emphasis on the two integral aspects of our business model: sales and how we can leverage those sales through systems.

You've probably heard me say many times that the most powerful aspect of our business model is how self-development is baked into the cake. We've done a great job of that. But to create a world-class organization, you have to be mindful about what kind of books, podcasts, seminars, and other development tools you're promoting through your team. If your emphasis is on training in areas like closing techniques, overcoming objections, and manipulative marketing tactics, that's certainly going to skew your recruiting and culture. If your self-development program encompasses more positive general development skills like health awareness, critical thinking, problem solving, relationship building, and communicating better, then you're going to ultimately have a stronger culture and overall team.

You don't grow your group. You grow your people—and they grow your group.

Every team has a prevailing ethos, and it is determined by the leaders at the top. It's worth some critical thinking about what kind of attitude and vibe you want your team to convey.

RECRUITING

Because of the preceding items, you already probably deduced that the integrity in your recruiting approach is vitally important. True. So let's look at some of the ways this could play out.

Let's begin with respect for your candidates, the choices they make, and their current situations. A disturbing trend in our business is "employee shaming." Becoming an entrepreneur is a choice, and it's not the right decision for everyone. Some people are more comfortable with (and better suited to) working for a company. Some of the jobs those people work will be at the entry or intermediate level. Treating those people like they're losers or underachievers doesn't demonstrate any integrity. (And shows you to be seriously deficient in the class department.)

A lot of people in our business who are still living in the past have created recruiting presentations demeaning formal education. While a college degree today comes with fewer possibilities for employment than ever before, it can be a wonderfully enriching experience for some. It certainly doesn't serve you or the profession to debase universities and colleges. (And the people who attend them.)

Every person in the world is important and wants to feel that way. Everyone deserves to be treated with respect. Let's not demean anyone's job or education. There's no integrity in that.

The other part of recruiting integrity is not making misleading product or income claims and testimonials. As a profession, we must continue to dramatically improve these practices or we will cease to exist. The regulatory bodies are simply not going to let things remain as they have been for decades. Every time someone on your team makes a dubious testimonial or claim, someone else is recording it on their phone or broadcasting it on the Internet. (Usually both.) It's just the new reality of the world today. Stuff that used to be said in a living room to six people is now seen and heard by 600. Which means a permanent record exists that can (and will) be used as evidence against you. There is no other choice but to change.

And I, for one, am delighted by this fact.

Because it's what we should be doing anyway. There is no place in our profession for laypeople to be making medical claims, offering diagnoses, or "prescribing" courses of treatment for medical conditions. There is no place in our profession for laypeople to be giving financial or investment advice. And there is no place in our profession for anyone to be making false, misleading, or exaggerated income claims.

Not only has the regulatory environment changed against these kinds of claims, but the marketplace has as well. People have become much more sophisticated, suspicious, and even jaded. When you watch some of the presentations from the dinosaurs still around, you'd think they learned them from Gordon Gecko in the movie *Wall Street*. It ain't the '80s anymore. Today, those hyped-up, rah-rah, get-rich-quick pitches actually repel more people than they attract. And more importantly, the people you actually want on your team are not the mouth-breathers impressed by the over-the-top sensationalism.

Imagine if you were considering a McDonald's, 7-Eleven, or a Subway franchise and you went for an exploratory visit to their corporate headquarters. Think about the presentation they would give you. They would probably detail the operational infrastructure they have in place to support their franchisees, the marketing system they would use to help promote you, and the hiring and training guidance they give; show you the breakdown of the financial rewards their people are achieving; and direct you to some of their happy and satisfied people. It would undoubtedly be very professional, business-like, and honest.

That's what we need to model. There's nothing wrong with having a call to action. (And many good reasons to include one.) But the more you imply that the timing for the opportunity is now, and the window is closing, the greater price you will pay later. If you have a legitimate opportunity, it should be just as great five years from now as it is today. That means you can make a compelling business-like presentation, just like one a successful franchise would make, without hype and pressure.

NOTE: We are *not* a franchise and there are very specific regulations to follow for franchising in most countries. I'm not suggesting you present your opportunity as a franchise investment. I'm simply saying that you can model the professional way they demonstrate their value—without using hype, exaggeration, or misrepresentation.

Another Important Element of Recruiting

One of the unique benefits that makes our business accessible for people, and also helps with its duplication, is the fact that it can be started part-time as a "side gig."

If you're recruiting by promoting five- and six-figure monthly incomes, you're negating one of the best benefits. The gig economy is sweeping the world, and technological developments will continue to increase that trend. Embrace the side gig concept and promote it. Of course, there will be ambitious people who succeed and graduate to full-time status with all of the perks that entails. But for the vast majority of your candidates, the side gig option is what they're looking for. And even those people seeking to make the business their main occupation should start it part-time on the side, continuing with whatever job or business they currently have.

Physical and Digital

Another consideration of your recruiting culture is more of an issue of how you set up your system, but deserves a quick mention here as well. Your recruiting materials all need to be available as both physical tools and digital tools. For the next few years, there will be a transition period as things move almost entirely into digital. But until then, your culture and system have to support those teams (especially in the developing world) who are not at the forefront of technology.

The first four or five people who join your team are going to be instrumental in how the culture and team develop. They may join because of a certain impetus, like getting in on the ground floor or because they hold you in such high regard. But what about recruit number 100? Or recruit number 1,000? Why should *she* join your team?

The best candidates actually don't need you or your opportunity. The best candidates always have many options to choose from, simply because of the nature of who they are. So...if you want to travel to Tibet, climb a mountain, meditate, and process one question with deep introspection, that would be this one:

Why should recruit number 1,000 join my team?

I can't give you that answer; it's something all great leaders must discern for themselves. But I can advise that you'd better figure it out. Because the short-term excitement of your first four or five close friends who joined because they're in your posse and think you're cool will not be enough to entice recruit number 1,000. The culture of your team is going to be the determining factor for that 1,000th recruit.

SELF-DEVELOPMENT

I told you in the last section that the best candidates don't really need you or your opportunity. When I sent a draft of this chapter to Wes Linden and Art Jonak, their comments were pretty telling. Wes wrote, "There are many good partners who come from the depths of despair. None of us three were rock stars when we joined." Art wrote, "IMO, the best candidates would probably not choose our business in its current state. I still believe the best candidate is the hungry one." Both of those comments illustrate an ironic aspect of the business...

Sometimes Your Worst Candidates Are Really Your Best Candidates

Wes is correct in the sense that you would not have wanted to sponsor him, Art, or me when each of us joined the business. In my case, I was probably the last guy on earth you'd want on your team. But in the case of all three of us, we turned out to become successful leaders in the end. This is the result of the value our profession puts on self-development as such an integral part of the business. The "perfect" candidates are harder to bring in, due to all the other options they have available to them. But there are many people (like the three of us were) who might look like lousy candidates to start, but who can be groomed into successful distributors if self-development is a fundamental tenet of your culture.

PACE OF GROWTH

Be quite mindful what kind of pace-of-growth culture you set early, because it's probably going to stick with you forever. Either you approach the business with a sense of urgency or you don't. I recommend the former.

Most compensation plans have one or two early ranks that don't require a great deal of accomplishment to achieve. Go after them fiercely. If you can reach the first one in a day or two, and the next one in a week or two, work hard to do that. Then you can set that vibe with your team. Example: "In our team, we have a culture of rapid rank advancement. I went Supervisor in my first 48 hours and want to help you do the same. And let's see if we can get you advanced to Manager in your first full week."

When you recognize and celebrate every rank advancement, no matter how minor, you build an environment that fosters more rank advancement. If you don't emphasize this, you create a culture of slow building, where rank advancements happen when they happen, not because people are mindfully seeking them.

Culture is being created constantly, one way or another, in many different areas. If you keep attention on these five main ones, you will ensure you have a team that operates with honesty, has strong duplication, and grows rapidly. (You also find that if you do a great job with these areas of culture, the minor ones generally fall into place.)

A team with strong culture will attract good people and produce great leaders. And when those good people show up, you want them to find a solid infrastructure in place. This includes a duplicable system, support materials, and proper training to guide them. And that's what we'll cover next.

CHAPTER 5

Building a Golden Goose (And Protecting Her)

Imagine you get a new Aston Martin coupe for your birthday. The suspension is fine-tuned, the engine has oodles of torque, and it corners as if gliding on rails. It's a beautiful and powerful machine, but that machine doesn't work in a vacuum. You need a dealership to handle maintenance and inventory spare parts. You need roads to drive on, hopefully with signage, lane markings, and traffic lights. You need to know there are service stations to refuel along the route. If that infrastructure were not there, that exquisite automobile would be worthless to you.

Think of your team infrastructure the same way. (And for the corporate execs reading this, your company infrastructure.) You can bring in the most talented people on the planet. But if you don't have a duplicable system, support materials, and training events to guide them, those people won't be able to achieve their true potential. It would be like driving your Aston Martin on a sandy beach.

This infrastructure gives your team a track to run on and provides some guardrails to keep them from driving off a cliff. Build it the right way and it will prevent you from having to experience a lot of extra DEFCON 1 situations down the road.

In terms of the big picture, you're building the golden goose. If you're not familiar with it, *The Goose That Laid the Golden Eggs* is one of the classic Aesop's Fables. It's the story of a goose that magically laid eggs of gold. Everything was going fabulously until the owner got greedy and cut open the goose to get all the golden eggs at once. To his dismay, he found no more eggs inside and the now dead goose would never produce another golden egg. The analogy here is that your company is the golden goose and must be protected at all costs. You do this with the infrastructure you create for the team.

PROCESS VERSUS IMPROVISATION

If there is an approved process to follow, team members will do so. If there isn't one, they will improvise their own, which can put the company at risk for lawsuits and regulatory actions. You need to ensure there are proper processes for new member orientations, the ladder of escalation in the recruiting pipeline, enrolling new customers and team members, and how someone becomes a part of team leadership.

Regarding the ladder of escalation, you also need to have specific marketing tools (audios, videos, catalogs, PDFs, etc.) for each stage in the process. Having distributors in the field who create their own marketing materials is extremely dangerous and a frequent cause of companies being targeted by regulators. (This situation is catnip for regulators.) Ideally, these materials should be developed by the company. But this development needs to be done in a true partnership with top field leaders. If your corporate team is unilaterally creating marketing without any consultation from the field, as a top field leader you may have to throw your weight around to get your (important and necessary) voice heard.

PUSH-AND-PULL PARTNERSHIPS

A lot of times, the final decisions on marketing materials are made by attorneys in the company's legal department. Most of them perceive their job to be covering their own ass, and so they veto any statement, claim, or benefit that could have even the most miniscule pushback from any regulator anywhere in the solar system. If you try to build a business with attorney-approved marketing materials, you're probably going to raise skinny children. The best materials result from a push-and-pull partnership between the field and legal to come up with something that is effective in the real world but does not pose such a high risk as to provoke regulatory or legal challenges.

Setting up these processes involves a tremendous amount of work in the beginning. But it saves you thousands of hours of work down the road. And more importantly, protects the golden goose.

If you are a top leader, one of the concepts I want you to obsess about is that of "compliance over perfection." You can design an airtight, totally regimented "perfect" system that pretty much no one is going to follow. Or you can design a system that is effective, but not perfect—and people actually follow it. (Read this paragraph twice. Then read it again. You just got your return on investment for buying this book.)

The three main objectives to be mindful of as you set up your system and materials are:

- How do we automate?
- How do we systematize?
- How do we scale?

Everything that can be automated should be automated. This ensures consistency and means the resource is available at any time. When processes are systematized, they facilitate better duplication. And if we want the best possible duplication, we definitely need to make sure things are scalable.

Allow me to share some real-world examples of "protecting the golden goose" in the day-to-day activity of building your team and growing your business.

One of the things you have to do as a leader is protect your sponsorship line and company executives while they are interacting with your team. This makes it easier for them to support your people and works to improve the likelihood that when they are looking for which teams they can visit, train, and encourage, they will think of yours first.

Suppose someone from your sponsorship line comes to town and conducts a mind-blowing, all-day training for your team. They even do a 60-minute Q&A session. What do you think happens the second they finish? They're surrounded by people who didn't have a peep to say during the Q&A session, but now are lined up to ask questions. (Sigh.)

Dozens or even hundreds more might want to take selfies. Sometimes the leaders need to be "rescued." One of your local leaders should sidle up to their ear and whisper, "Do you need to be rescued?" If they answer affirmatively, get them out of there gracefully without making them the bad guy or gal. Say something like, "Marianne has been very gracious with her time, but right now she must fulfill some other commitments. I'm afraid I need to steal her away." Then take her by the arm and guide her out of the room to the elevator, running interference along the way.

If an audience is larger than 300 people, the speaker may not be able to take questions or selfies. Check with them in advance, learn their preferences, then honor them. (Sometimes they may want to engage with your people longer, but they've been on stage for two hours and desperately need a bathroom break first!)

When the speaker does agree to stay for questions, take selfies, or sign books, arrange some volunteers to manage the process. Simple things like instructing people to have their phone cameras ready or someone on hand to take their pic, directing them to have the book opened to the signing page before they reach the front of the line, and keeping the line moving along can make a huge difference in the experience for everyone involved.

I like to assign a personal host/guide to take care of every high-level visitor for their entire stay. The host picks them up at the airport and transfers them to the hotel. During the ride the host inquires what the guest would like to happen during their stay. Would they like to see any sights while they are there? Did they forget to pack something? Do they want to meet or dine with top leaders or just lie low?

We have the guest already checked into the hotel, room paid for, with bottled water and refreshments waiting inside. The guest of honor is able to skip the check-in hassles and go directly to their room to unwind. (Or go shopping, take a tour of the town, get a massage, or anything else they've indicated they would like to do.) We even have a nice thank you card waiting for them in their room, hand-signed by the local leaders. (And if I'm being totally honest here, probably some gaudy local souvenirs.)

Suppose your company president agrees to speak at one of your major events. I can guarantee you that at some point a distributor will roll up on them with a pressing monumental issue. (Like the bottle of 60-count vitamins they received had only 59 capsules in it, or the banana-flavored protein shake has bananas in it, and their cousin Hugo is allergic to bananas.) You need to make sure a leader takes the offending distributor around the shoulder and offers to assist them in getting their problem solved with the appropriate department of the company. Protect your execs.

When You Build the Culture and Infrastructure Right, You Make Your Team the One Everyone Wants to Work With.

Let me give you a perfect example of how this plays out in the field. When the company I was working with first launched Russia, predictably there were some logistical and operational issues.

To help sort things out and support the new market, the company would send the president or CEO and several VPs to my major events there. At the first of these events, I set up a dinner afterward, including the execs and about 10 of my Russian leaders. Before the waiter had a chance to even bring the drinks, my top guy started grilling the execs about some inventory issues. The execs politely addressed his concerns. But my guy was just getting warmed up. He moved on to another issue. And then another. Then his people started joining in about the challenges they were facing. It turned into a three-hour bitch session. I allowed this to go on, because I was frustrated myself and wanted to make sure that the execs really understood what their actions (or lack of them) were doing to stymie growth in the field. But everyone involved left the dinner feeling like they had been through the wringer.

Fast forward four months later. Another major event, a different group of executives, but pretty much the same result. One problem comes up, gets discussed, then the next, and the next, and the next... What had been initiated as an after-event appreciation dinner had turned into a torture chamber for the execs. (A torture chamber augmented by bleak Soviet-style architecture, exhausting jet lag, and the subzero Russian winter.) I'm sure they never wanted to come back to Moscow again.

Fast forward four months later. Another major event. Once we had all arrived at the restaurant, I began with an announcement. I thanked the executives for agreeing to come to speak at the event and explained how grateful we were for their efforts. Then I asked to go around the table and for each distributor share their "why"—the reason they joined the business and what their dreams are. It's a moving experience and many people get emotional. The execs start to see that my team is not a bunch of mean people who want to "catch" them doing bad things—but is actually made up of good, passionate people who are seeking success for the right reasons.

Next, I announce that there will be no more business talk allowed. We are only going to be social and get to know each other better. I ask the execs to share where they're from and tell us about their families. It's a wonderful experience and again, some people are tearing up. Now my people see the execs are not mean bureaucrats conspiring in cubicles on how to make the business more difficult—but are good people who have spouses, children, and dreams just like they do. True relationships and a partnership developed, and the market went on to produce millions of dollars in sales every month.

Make sure you understand the human dynamics of what happened here. It's just human nature that when a distributor gets a chance to engage with corporate, they'll probably have some problem or challenge they would like to see resolved. And there will always be some issues needing attention. But once the pattern was set after the first few dinners, I could see they would become arduous bitch-fests every time thereafter. And that rarely produces solutions for real issues. By breaking that destructive pattern and implementing a better one, we created a positive mutual working arrangement where solutions came about.

Most distributors have a default position: They think if the ignorant company execs would just charge less money for the products and pay more money into the comp plan, the company would become the most successful one in history.

Most executives have a default position: They think if the lazy distributors would just sponsor more frequently and sell more products, the company would become the most successful one in history.

They're Both Wrong.

The field believes the corporate team doesn't really understand what happens in the field, what makes a candidate join the team, and how business is actually produced.

The corporate team believes the field doesn't really understand what goes into product costs, pricing, manufacturing, finance, human resources, IT, and all of what it takes to keep the business operating.

This Time, They're Both Right.

A big part of what makes the golden goose the golden goose is a mutually beneficial partnership between the field and corporate. To paraphrase Stephen Covey, if you want to be understood, seek first to understand. One of your most important jobs as a top leader is facilitating a positive and empowering relationship between the field and corporate. Both groups must work together to protect the golden goose.

Most of us are seeking that elusive animal known as *exponential growth*. The magic that happens when an organization goes into this type of hyper growth is one of the most breathtaking experiences I've enjoyed in my career. But it can't happen unless the culture is correct, the infrastructure is built, and there is a strong working relationship between field and corporate. In Chapter 6, we'll look at the other necessary elements that create exponential growth.

CHAPTER 6

Creating Momentum and Exponential Growth

Sounds crazy, but it's true. It is easier to build your business fast than to build slow. Just as you frequently witness in sports, momentum begets more momentum, and sometimes an unstoppable force is created.

Know what it's like to check your back office and see more than 4,000 new team members with activation orders—in a day? And then more than 4,000 the next day? And the next? And the next?

I do.

Know what it's like to see those tens of thousands of new team members go inactive and disappear because the company couldn't handle the demand and ship their first orders?

I do.

Everyone talks about that magical, mythical animal known as "exponential growth." It's almost impossible to find a recruiting presentation that doesn't have a Power-Point slide showing a chart with a hockey stick line of steady growth suddenly curving dramatically toward the

65

heavens, then disappearing into the top right corner of the chart. But most people have never actually been a part of true exponential growth.

I have. Twice.

Once it worked elegantly, because the company was prepared and had the resources to handle the massive spike in demand. Another time was the scenario described above, where the hard work of amazing leaders was squandered and reputations were destroyed, with pain and chaos the result.

EXPONENTIAL GROWTH IS NOT A FANTASY

As leaders, we have a sacred responsibility to provide sound advice and helpful mentoring to our people, guiding them to the most effective and productive ways to grow their business. Exponential growth is not a fantasy. It can really occur. If there is any possibility that your company can hit and sustain itself through an exponential growth cycle, you must do everything in your power to make this happen. And if your company doesn't look like it is tracking toward exponential growth, you should look for the reasons why.

Exponential growth gets into your blood. And the only thing that takes it out is embalming fluid. After my experience in this area, I would be remiss if I didn't share with you the dynamics you must have in place if you desire to create this kind of growth. There are five foundational elements.

1) A Sexy Product Story

Did I mention the story needs to be sexy?

- Your multivitamin has 88 percent of the recommended daily allowance? (Yawn.)
- Your protein powder has 7 percent more grams per serving than your competitor? (Wake me up when you're done.)
- You're launching a new product with CBD oil? (You're putting me into a coma here...)

There are literally *hundreds* of companies in the Leveraged Sales space with stories similar to those. We're looking for a story that captures the imagination of the public, something that generates water cooler conversation. In this age of overwhelming white noise, you need social media virality to even get into the discussion. This means having a story that the average person "gets," one that powerfully illustrates how your product will enhance their life in a way they find desirable. Something fresh, compelling, and captivating.

2) A Dynamic Executive Team

Start with a rock star CEO, president, or founder. You need at least one. Someone charismatic who can present on stage in a way that intrigues candidates and inspires distributors. If your founder is a nerdy scientist in a lab coat with coke-bottle glasses and a social anxiety disorder, you better have a CEO or president who can be the front person. I'm not saying this to taunt people with social anxiety (I suffer from it myself) or to be snarky. The Supremes had Diana Ross, Guns N' Roses has Axl, and U2 has Bono. Every company that cuts through the clutter to hit exponential growth has a dynamo like Mark Hughes, Mary Kay Ash, or A.L. "Art" Williams Jr. rocking the stage and the Internet.

Then this rock star needs a powerful team. You want a mix of people with extensive industry experience who know where the bodies are buried and brash newcomers without preconceived perceptions on everything. (Or maybe more correctly, anything.) That means a brilliant chief technology officer (CTO), marketing people who actually understand our profession, a superb customer service manager, and an outstanding COO who can deliver lockdown logistics. Oh, and a CFO who really comprehends comp plan analysis, cost of goods, and cash flow. Which leads us to the next foundational element.

3) Lots and Lots of Money

Back in the day, companies used to try to entice distributors with tales of their homespun, started-from-a-dining-room-table history. A very quaint concept, but one that pretty much guarantees failure in the current market reality. While technology has reduced the amount of start-up capital required to launch a business today, it has also erased borders and made the whole world a village. A company that starts up in only one country today will face a sizable market disadvantage from the beginning.

The investment required for international operations is substantial if you actually do it legally and correctly.

The type of executive team I described above doesn't come cheap. I've seen more than a couple companies that started with initial investments of three to five million dollars run out of money and close down. And a few that started with ten million dollars that suffered the same fate. Everyone likes to spotlight the plucky entrepreneurs who started with almost nothing and bootstrapped their way to success. Deservedly so, because these people justify the respect they engender. But they are outliers and not indicative of what succeeds most of the time. There's a saying in boxing: "The biggest guy doesn't always win, but that's the way to bet." With companies, the way to bet is on the one with lots of cash.

4) A Compensation Plan That Promotes Healthy Growth

Creating the right comp plan is one of the most nuanced, complex, and perplexing projects to tackle. Yet this is an area on which most new companies spend the least amount of time. Most of them just mimic the plan they see someone else operating successfully, simply changing the rank titles and a percentage or two. This is a horrific idea because comp plans are not "one size fits all." They are greatly influenced by what kind of products are offered, how many, their price structure, and the amount of ongoing consumption they generate. Each company must employ a very delicate and precise science to design an effective plan that does the most important thing: promote healthy growth.

I wrote an extremely detailed breakdown of comp plan design in *Direct Selling Success*, so I won't repeat it here. But to create exponential growth, your plan needs to reward people for doing the right behavior: developing a customer base and working down in the group. If your plan rewards bad behavior like frontloading new people with expensive activation orders to get fast-start bonuses or just concentrating on personal enrollments, you'll create initial movement, then stall out, and never enter momentum.

Let's say a company has all four of these elements in spades. They still have no chance of hitting momentum without the fifth element. Because no matter how amazing your product is, no matter how dynamic the corporate team is, no matter how much money you have, no matter how supercalifragilisticexpialidocious your comp plan is—no company has ever put itself into exponential growth. Or ever will. Because momentum can only be created by...

5) A Strong Field Leadership Team

The kind of culture buzz that creates exponential growth is created in the field by field leaders. Leaders who operate with impeccable integrity, model the right behavior, provide true system and infrastructure support to their team, and put in the necessary effort and work. In other words, the kind of leader who does the things we're talking about in this book.

The momentum that produces exponential growth is simply the action of scaling your integrity, support, and leadership so it can reach a vast swath of people.

True exponential growth is never produced by a single leader, no matter how powerful she is. It requires a diverse leadership team that reflects the makeup of the population, one that works together to create a finished product—the system—which is greater than anything any one individual could produce themselves. For that reason, I encourage you to create study groups and trainings with your key leaders around chapters in this book.

I worked for over a decade in a company in which the Diamond Director pin was the highest award series of ranks you could attain. And when you reached the first Diamond rank, they treated you like royalty. They put your picture on billboards in your hometown, flew you from the airport to the events in a helicopter, and basically created a documentary story of your life to play at the annual convention when you received your pin. They honestly treated you with more reverence and respect than some prime ministers receive on state visits. As a kid who was expelled from high school, I found these experiences to be some of the most exhilarating moments in in my life.

And when you're on the receiving end of that kind of admiration, devotion, and veneration, you can get pretty used to that. You've reached an inner circle that you don't ever want to be left out of again. (Proof that the recognition program is always more powerful than the money.) The high you get from this royal treatment is one you always seek to maintain. It keeps you focused on staying qualified and achieving yet higher levels of accomplishment.

And since I'm being so transparent with you in this manual, I can tell you that not getting this treatment at every event can also give you a little twinge of jealousy.

Here's why: As you work your way up the career path, the distance between ranks gets harder and harder to achieve. Whereas at the lower stages of a comp plan you might advance by increasing from 200 points a week to 400 points, at the top levels, the jump might be from one million points to two million, or two million to four million. At the elite reaches of the compensation plan, no one keeps breaking new ranks every single year. (Company executives, please read that last sentence again.) You can still be duplicating with your team and volume increasing but not break a new rank from one convention to the next.

So it's pretty easy to be sitting in the front row, feeling a little diminished and forsaken, as other leaders walk across the stage, captivating the convention with their tales of triumph and being lavished with praise and recognition. I was the number one income earner worldwide for seven years running. Yet there were still times I felt petty and jealous, being left out of the spotlight after all I had accomplished.

That isn't a great demonstration of leadership. (It is, however, a perfect demonstration of what being human looks like.) But of course, our mission is to become the highest possible versions of ourselves. And what happened next was the culmination of that.

Because as I evolved, something fascinating started to occur. I stopped craving the stage recognition for myself. Instead, it was replaced with the joy that comes from seeing your people—the leaders you have developed—receiving their due up on that stage. And you get to be in the front row as they are recognized for the exemplary leaders they have developed into.

You've probably heard me say often that your most important job is to work yourself out of a job. And when you are reveling in seeing your leaders getting their just rewards, you know that you've done your job—which is creating a strong field leadership team that can outlive you.

As you're developing your culture, designing your system, and building your infrastructure, keep this potential result of exponential growth in your mind. Since it's easier to build fast than it is to build slow, and it's a lot more fun to build big than to build tiny, do your best to facilitate momentum.

If you do have all five of these elements in place, you're positioned to create robust growth. But first you're going to have to overcome many difficulties—the kind created by egoists, toxic people, crossline cancers, and competitors who want to drive you out of business. (Not to mention zombies, dinosaurs, parasites, and terrorists.) The kind of difficulties that require DEFCON 1 preparedness. And that's what we will unpack next.

CHAPTER 7

Dangerous Field Dynamics and How to Solve Them

I warned you that you're going to have to overcome many difficulties—the kind created by egoists, toxic people, crossline cancers, and just all-around negative and disruptive people. Some of these people will be on your team, some will be crossline, others will be in corporate, and yet others will be competitors. Some of this behavior will be people practicing self-sabotage, some of it will be well meaning but harmful, and some of it will be consciously directed to cause you to fail. Our business is driven by people. And people are sometimes kind, thoughtful, and gracious, and sometimes petty, jealous, and nasty. As a result, these people create situations that require DEFCON 1 preparedness on your part. Your job as a leader involves many ways in which you will interact with those people and situations.

Some of the objectives great leaders strive to accomplish are:

- Helping people overcome their own limiting beliefs and self-destructive behavior

- Challenging their people to become the highest possible version of themselves
- Resolving conflicts created by jealousy, ego, and "sibling rivalry" between lines
- Protecting the team from dinosaurs, zombies, parasites, and terrorists
- Keeping communication and partnership open between corporate and the field
- Enforcing the death penalty to remove dangerous people who threaten the golden goose

In this chapter, we'll explore how you handle difficulties that occur in the field from your team, crossline teams, and competitors in other companies. In later chapters we'll look at the best ways to respond to challenges from corporate, government regulators, and other forces outside your control.

CROSSLINE NAVIGATION

Let's begin the discussion with a look at working with multiple lines. This is an essential skill every successful leader must master. Back in the day, things were simpler because we just maintained a policy that "no business should go crossline." If you had sponsored Pete and Elizabeth, and they saw each other at team events, they might engage in some friendly social banter, but they'd never discuss anything related to the business. Today, with the construction of comp plans, lines are not so clearly delineated. You might sponsor 15 personal enrollees, but they are all in one or two common lines. (Then of course, just to really keep it interesting, you have lines of people who are not anywhere in your team, but in the lines of others. In a sense, they are cross-crossline.) As a result, it sometimes gets messy. Very messy. There really is no way to prevent this, just ways to keep it manageable. Some better than others.

There are many support functions like training, where the most productive approach is to work with the whole team. (Or different crosslines or even the entire company working together, like at an annual convention.) And just like in families, sometimes sibling rivalries develop between lines. A big part of your success will come from learning when you can engage with multiple lines versus when you need to isolate one line. And what to do when the lines interact on their own in ways that are not beneficial to everyone involved. Let's explore some examples and how to best respond.

A Rogue Leader Unplugs from the Team

This is probably the most frequent issue you'll encounter. And it's problematic. Usually a move like this is driven by ego issues and these are difficult to resolve, as the party involved believes they are faultless, and the universe revolves around them. They get a taste of being featured on the platform and broadcasts, and they become intoxicated with the fame, adulation, and glory. They decide the best thing for their team would be if, leadership-wise, they were pretty much the only offering on the menu.

This is messy, because each person in the team has the prerogative to do this. They are working their own business and their own income. From their viewpoint, everyone in the team comes from the lineage of the people they personally sponsored, so in one sense, they've built the whole team. This is sometimes true—and sometimes wildly delusional. Often the primary reason the organization grew and prospered was because there were people up the sponsorship line who came down and worked in the group. (Not to mention, in many current plans, the sponsorship line actually does place people beneath you.) And the existing infrastructure of training, tools, events, and the system play integral roles.

But for whatever reason, whether valid or not, a leader decides to unplug. They break away to host their own events and promote their own system. This presents a situation that will require you to be delicate and nuanced.

You do not want to publicly de-edify the rogue leader. If you do, you'll push them away forever and spread negativity within the group. But you don't necessarily want to publicly endorse their actions, because that would send a confusing message to the rest of the team. The dicey part is most likely to come because you are approached by people in the affected team who desire to remain with the bigger group and not break away. While they are in the rogue leader's team, they are also in yours, and you have a responsibility to help them. You should allow them to participate in your events and infrastructure and do so without saying anything negative about the unplugged leader. Your perfect outcome would be that the unplugged person or people will eventually see the wisdom of rejoining the bigger team. If that doesn't happen, and often it doesn't, your fallback goal is to keep the rogue leader and their people in the company, peacefully coexisting, instead of their leaving for another opportunity.

THE LEADER IS A TOXIC PERSON

Most people fear confrontation and like to tell everyone what they want to hear. That works for surviving politics in a corporate cubicle war, but it doesn't work for leading a team or accomplishing anything worthwhile. Toxicity never just goes away. It rots and festers, infecting everything around it. And toxic people are energy vampires. They go around with a metaphorical set of jumper cables, hoping to latch onto anyone they meet and suck all of the energy out of their body. They are "locker room cancers" on a team and need to be addressed. You have to tackle the toxins.

The first course of action is always gentle persuasion. Most negative people have no idea they are negative. Seriously. They really don't. (I sure didn't realize I was.) They think they're being realistic, contrarian, or "telling it like it is." In reality, they can find the cloud in every silver lining. Encourage them to participate more actively in self-development and personal growth. Recommend specific books about persuasion, relationships, and communication that will help them improve. (Examples: *How to Win Friends & Influence People*, by Dale Carnegie, and *The Go-Giver Influencer*, by Bob Burg and John David Mann.)

If that doesn't work, you've got to dial up the focus through your monthly counseling with them. This may require actually telling them that they are coming off as negative and toxic and are diminishing the positive potential results with their customers and team members. Don't do this in a way to "catch" them or beat them down. Do this in a spirit of empathy and genuinely wanting to help them reach a breakthrough. Hopefully they receive this as the helpful wake-up call it is meant to be and will respond appropriately.

In rare cases, they take such feedback poorly and become defensive or even abusive, and their behavior spirals downward. If this gets too extreme, you might have to excommunicate them from your team events and platform. This is a Draconian step and should be done only as a last resort. But if the situation requires such action, do it. Nothing kills a team faster than a toxic person with an all-access pass.

Sometimes you are dealing with people who have serious mental health issues or personality disorders. Here are some tips for identifying these people:

- They are extremely charismatic and focus their attention on you and make you feel special. When you are no longer valuable to them, they repeat the behavior with someone else.

- They are narcissists, with a grandiose sense of self-importance. Narcissists believe they are "special" and can only be understood by other special people. They are too good to be restricted by any rules or norms the team has.

- They never reveal much personal info about themselves except to *tell* you who they are. Example: "I am so empathetic that if you cut, I bleed." Well-adjusted people don't need to advertise who they are; they let their lives demonstrate it.

- They have tons of time to talk about what they want but aren't interested in listening to you.

They will exploit or hurt others without any guilt, in order to preserve the view of themselves they are cultivating.

- They have a strong sense of entitlement. They demand special treatment and expect the trappings of higher ranks even if they haven't achieved them.

- They leave a lot of dead bodies behind them in the form of people quitting their team, and they don't really have friends in the business.

People in this category are way above your pay grade and can't be coached; they require a trained mental health counselor. You must excommunicate them from your team events and platform as described above. **Note:** These situations requiring excommunication should be rare. Exceedingly rare. If they're not, and you are experiencing a lot of them, it means your culture is deficient and requires serious work. Good culture should cause these people to self-deport from the team. **Note to the Note:** If you're sure the team culture is adequate and you are still experiencing a lot of toxic, dysfunctional people who need to be excommunicated, *you* might actually be the person needing a mental health professional.

😑 😑 😑

THE LEADER HAS LOW SELF-ESTEEM AND DOESN'T WANT TO BE RECOGNIZED IN THE GROUP

Some people believe that staying off the stage demonstrates their humility. Others are just extra shy or introverted and think they can hang back and let other people be the face of the team. You have to show them that this behavior ultimately harms their business. Their team wants and needs to see them as part of leadership. There is a real feeling of "pride of ownership" involved. People don't want to follow followers; they want to follow leaders. Work with your introverted types to gradually up their exposure. Don't frighten them out of the business. But challenge them to grow incrementally.

Your Sponsor Lacks Integrity

This is a tough one. And like a lot of these issues, how you respond needs to be determined in nuanced degrees. Maybe your sponsor is one of the old-school dinosaurs who thinks all recruiting is done with hype and breathless sensationalism. You might hold your nose but decide it's not a hill to die on.

Now let's suppose they're worse than a dinosaur—they're making outrageous income or product claims that threaten the golden goose. Or maybe they're a zombie who jumps companies and is always shopping around for a better deal. The first step would be to talk to them one on one and express your concerns. If that doesn't produce the right result, then escalate the conversation up the sponsorship line. And by escalate, I mean be an adult. Be willing to have a conversation with your sponsor and the upline sponsor and say exactly what the offending behavior is. Any kind of unethical behavior threatens your business, so this is not the time to be meek. And if the sponsorship line cannot resolve the situation, take it to the company.

Suppose your sponsor (or someone in the sponsorship line) actually steals recruits or even team members from others in the group (or from other groups). They're trying to cross-recruit illegal pyramids within the team, or preying on team members by selling $5,000 coaching sessions, or running a cocaine ring in the group. (No joke, this actually happens.) Immediately escalate this to the company or, in the case where you are personally exposed to illegal activity, notify the authorities. (And then immediately notify the company of the entire situation.)

In all cases, if the offending behavior is not resolved, you will be left with three choices: Number one, unplug from the sponsor and begin your own culture and system. This involves a tremendous amount of work. Literally years, in some cases. The second option is to resign and be inactive for the required time until you can start over and enroll with another sponsor. (These waiting periods are generally from six months to one year.) Your third option is to resign and find another company to join, one where the sponsor and values are aligned with yours (which we will explore deeper in Chapter 12). Over the course of my almost 40 years in the profession, I've had to implement both options one and three. None of them are easy or fun. But your integrity is at stake and doing the right thing matters. A lot.

By the way, this may sound crazy, but the fact that your sponsor makes a post on social media supporting a candidate in the political party you hate does not mean they are an evil monster with no integrity. It just means they have a different political view than you do.

TWO LEADERS IN A "CIVIL WAR" TRY TO GET THEIR TEAMS INVOLVED

This is a textbook example of why the "cut off your nose to spite your face" cliché became a cliché. There is nothing more destructive to a team than taking negativity down the group. I don't mince words with these situations. Get both parties together in a room with you and issue an ultimatum. Demand all public negativity stop instantly or they will be removed from the leadership team. And if the negativity continues in a way that threatens the golden goose, let them know you will go to the company and demand the offending distributor(s) be terminated (as I discussed in an earlier chapter). Getting in the middle of this kind of drama is messy and uncomfortable. But it's a situation of needing to cut out the tumor if you want to save the patient.

A DISTRIBUTOR LACKS SUPPORT AT HOME...

...and calls to say they have received an ultimatum: "Either the marriage or the business." Talk about walking a tightrope. Truth is, though, this kind of conflict comes up a lot. Your job is to keep the situation from getting to this breaking point. Some things that help in this regard: First, do not create pressure or "guilt trip" the spouse or partner who is not enamored with the business. Our business is unconventional and threatens the status quo in many ways, which means we have a lot of people and institutions attacking us. This has created a negative reputation in some corners. *And* we've had a lot of unscrupulous people who have practiced a lot of sleazy, sketchy tactics for a long time. This has also created a negative reputation in some corners. So when we encounter people who are skeptical, cynical, and/or negative about our business, let's give them the benefit of the doubt, deploy some empathy, and understand how their opinion might have come about.

This is another example of why I gave you the earlier advice about not holding regular team social events. If you have someone working the business three evenings a week already, and then you have them join your team's poker game on Friday nights, of course their partner is going to resent the competition for their time.

The best cure for this is to meet and get to know the nonparticipating spouses or partners. Especially helpful is if you can get them to attend a major event. Major events really impact people in an affirmative way because of the positive energy they have and the belief they create. Make sure that at your major events you celebrate and recognize *both* spouses.

There are two top-secret, thermonuclear weapons that will eventually win over a skeptical partner or spouse, and they fall into the reward and recognition department: bonus cars and award trips. Help your team member with a skeptical partner qualify for a bonus car or a free trip to Hawaii in the wintertime, and I promise you, their negative spouse will be instantly transformed into a born-again evangelical proponent of the business.

A LEADER IS PROMOTING SKETCHY, OFF-SYSTEM WEBINARS OR EVENTS TO THE TEAM

Picture this scenario: Juan, one of your directors, gets invited to a workshop from His Holiness, Prema Baba Swami Salami. Swami Salami used to be Ed, who sold data plans at the AT&T store until one evening when he ingested some peyote and found himself levitated into the Astral Plane, where he happened to meet Jesus, Gandhi, and the Buddha. Ed says that these spiritual leaders anointed him to swami status and sent him back to earth to minister to the masses. Your guy Juan attends the swami's workshop at the Holiday Inn and believes he has discovered the true meaning of intergalactic cosmic connection. Now Juan is promoting the swami's $15,000 introductory workshop to all of the people on your team.

Or Melissa, one of your new distributors who hasn't earned her first 100 dollars yet, takes an incredible $297 online seminar that promises enrollees they will learn how to build a Leveraged Sales business by running Facebook ads. The person who conducts the seminar has never built a Leveraged Sales business and knows nothing about duplication, but Melissa is positive it's a peachy keen idea. So, although she hasn't actually, you know, sponsored anyone, she starts promoting the online seminar to the other members of your team.

Or Pierre, one of your top leaders, attends a seminar taught by an expert. Unfortunately, a lot of the "experts" today are zombies or dinosaurs who have become irrelevant in the business. Now they make their living selling generic training to you and your team. This expert offers expensive coaching programs and retreats costing anywhere from $5K to $25K. Pierre participates and becomes so enamored promoting the products from this expert that his own business actually starts trending downward.

In all of these scenarios, and many similar ones, a cardinal rule of our business is being broken. That rule is "Never mess with anyone else's income."

If you attend the *How to Have a Metaphysically Woke Inner Child and Cosmically Coagulate Your Chakras* workshop, and you think it's transformational, that's certainly your prerogative. But when you recommend that workshop to the distributors on Jerry's team, now you're messing with Jerry's income. His people could stop attending his major events, because their time, attention, and money are diverted to outside activities. Leaders work exceptionally hard to present enough events to provide the training their team needs, without overwhelming them to the point where it has a negative rather than positive effect on their business. They are not going to appreciate an outsider messing up that dynamic.

It's important that your training and culture include the "Never mess with anyone else's income" philosophy. When people start promoting training events or tools crossline, you have to immediately shut them down. You shouldn't be recommending any business-building tools or events (including this book) outside your own line. Mind your own business and stay out of other people's.

You've Sponsored Someone Who Is a Distraction Factory

Humans are funny creatures. People say they join the business because they want to be successful. Then, when they are given a choice between doing the work that will make them successful or engaging in a distraction, a large percentage of them opt for the cat videos.

In this business, we make money one way, and one way only: Get a customer to buy our product or service. This happens two ways, and two ways only: You put someone in front of a presentation, and they buy. Or you recruit someone to be a distributor and teach that person how to put someone in front of a presentation so they can buy. *We get paid only when the product or service reaches the end consumer.*

Suzie has the option of calling the best people on her candidate list to attend the next presentation. Or she could watch the streaming feed of a competitor to "check out what they are doing." Which activity do you think she's going to choose?

Part of your job as a leader is to practice "tough love" and keep directing people back to the work they need to be doing for their success. Your people will contact you with pressing emergencies like why the new label on the energy bars is green instead of red, or why the point value on the dish soap changed from 12PV to 11PV. They will want to gossip about what another line or another company is doing. They will want to debate the potential of the technique some zombie or dinosaur is suggesting in the e-course they are pitching on Instagram. They will want to debate the percentages paid on a certain level of the comp plan or editorialize on the location the company chooses for the award trip. They will believe the two hours a night they spend watching cats on vacuums and dogs on surfboards count as building their candidate list or conducting market research.

You have to kill distractions like a ninja!

When your people contact you in the situations above—and the 107,346,222 others exactly like them—you have to kill that distraction and direct them back to the Prime Directive (aka *Starfleet General Order 1*):

Get candidates in front of a marketing presentation so they can make the best decision for them.

Meeting people, working your candidate list, inviting and hosting presentations are "rainmaker" activities in alignment with the Prime Directive. Any other activity is busywork.

The Leader Is Easily Distracted or Off System

The most sacred place in your organization is the platform: the events, both live and online, that are facilitated by the team leaders. Any time you feature someone on one of these events, there is an implied endorsement that what they speak is true and correct. So if someone loses the plot and starts promoting anything off system, you have to shut that down immediately. Explain again the system and what is expected of them. If they don't understand, open this book to this paragraph and show them. If they still are unable to stay on system, you must remove them from the public platforms.

A Team Member Is Recruiting for Another Opportunity

This is actually one of those situations that has both a protocol and also legal considerations. Let's say you've enrolled Rex. Rex then sponsors Matthew, Mark, Luke, and John. Those four guys are Rex's personal enrollees. Because Rex is an independent contractor and these enrollees are his personals, if he wants to also try to recruit them into another company, or another 10 companies, he has the legal right to do that. (And this is considered ethical protocol in the profession. Not *smart*, but still ethical.) You may not agree with this or like it, but you have no recourse. (This is Rex's income and you don't get to mess with it.)

But let's go down another level. Matthew sponsors Sarah. Rex *does not* have the legal right to approach her. (And most company P&Ps would also prohibit this.) Likewise, if Matthew approaches any crossline distributors, he would have no legal or ethical justification for doing this.

Cross-recruiting for another opportunity is a dangerous and harmful practice and should be dealt with immediately and forcefully, usually by termination. People who attempt to build more than one program simultaneously are never successful. So there is no long-term loss in terminating someone who does this. On the other hand, not terminating them and allowing them to infect others with this behavior is extremely harmful long-term.

ONE OR MORE TOP LEADERS LEAVE TO JOIN ANOTHER COMPANY

This situation can become devastating or negligible—or land somewhere in between. A huge part of retention is the social proof and belief demonstrated by the field leaders in a company. When a top leader or several of them quit to join another company, that departure can send shock waves through the team. Frequently, team members will have thoughts like "If (top leader) Stuart, who makes gobs of money, doesn't believe in the company any longer, what chance do I have? What does he know that I don't?"

This situation has a lot in common with parents revealing to their children that they are getting divorced. If the parents are negative and panicky, the kids are going to be petrified. (And probably at least a little scared, no matter how the parents handle it.) The way you and the other remaining leaders respond to the defections plays a deciding role in how damaging the departures are. This is where all of your hard work supporting your team (or not supporting them) will bear fruit.

Let's talk about how this scenario should be handled. Just as in the cross-recruiting scenario, there is an accepted protocol here: If someone leaves a company for any reason, they have every right to speak with their personal enrollees to let them know why they're leaving. They can even ask their enrollees to leave with them. But if they approach others in the team, or members in other lines, they are now acting unethically, should be terminated if they haven't already left, and possibly face legal action.

How you respond to these situations is going to depend on how the departing leader is conducting her- or himself. If they leave in an ethical manner, give them the respect they deserve. There need be no shame in people leaving. Radio DJs quit working for *Hot 105* to work for *97 JAMZ* and vice versa, and execs leave Burger King go to work for McDonald's and vice versa.

A few years ago, a company approached a couple who were high-level leaders on my team. The company wanted them to relaunch the United States under a new brand for them. As much as I hated to see them go, I also celebrated that they had progressed into such good leaders that other companies wanted to recruit them. As I told my team, I feel honored that my "coaching tree" has developed into so many companies over the years. They have done well, I've done well, and we're still friends to this day.

Earlier I told you the story about the time my sponsor jumped ship to join another company. When that happened, not a single person on my team left with him. I had spent years working down in depth in their groups, conducting trainings, doing monthly counseling, and just being supportive and accessible overall. I had commiserated with them during tragedies and celebrated births, graduations, and victories. We had a relationship that superseded external factors.

Other Times It's Not So Seamless

Sometimes people leave with a scorched-earth strategy, publicly and privately spreading disparaging statements, innuendoes, and outright lies. The company they've been working with and getting paid by for years, magically and seemingly overnight, is transformed into a den of inequity, run by sleazebags, con artists, and criminals. When you face this kind of attack, you must respond quickly and decisively. Do not respond in kind. But understand that someone who does this is a threat and is doing everything they can to drive you out of business. Don't let accusations go unanswered.

In cases like this, it's always better if your team first learns about it from you, framed in the right context. My default setting is first to say something like "Edward and Rachel have decided to resign and go with another company. I wish them success in their new endeavor." I want to keep things positive. But if they start with lies and attacks, I will respond forcefully, acknowledging my profound disappointment that they have chosen to go the negative route and refuting any lies or misrepresentations they make.

If you do have someone depart and make negative attacks, record their livestreams and take screenshots of stuff they post online. Send this evidence immediately to your company's legal department. They need to issue stern warnings about the legal consequences of slander and libel, and if the offending party doesn't cease immediately, file restraining orders and/or lawsuits.

Note: Be smart ahead of time. If you find out someone is leaving for another company, or even if you think they're a flight risk, act to remove their access to member emails, the team website, and moderator status on team social media accounts. Don't wait until they do a Facebook Live to the entire team about why your company suddenly sucks before revoking their admin status in the Facebook group.

If you are a strong, positive leader, and you're doing the work we're discussing in this book, you won't experience a major hit when leaders jump to another company. The people who leave usually just take the low-hanging fruit—unsuccessful people at the bottom of the comp plan who see a shot at stardom somewhere else.

As you've already discovered, this is a long chapter. These are just the DEFCON 1 scenarios you must prepare for that come from inside your own company. And just from the field. We haven't even discussed corporate yet. Not to mention, there is a whole world of zombies, dinosaurs, parasites, and terrorists outside your team and company that can create DEFCON 1 emergencies for you. And that's what we'll explore next.

CHAPTER 8

Protecting Your Team Against Zombies, Dinosaurs, Parasites, and Terrorists

Think back to when you saw that first presentation and decided to join the business. I'm betting you had no idea you were going to have to defend yourself against zombies, dinosaurs, parasites, and terrorists. It sounds like a convoluted mix of science fiction, historical documentaries, medical shows, and action thrillers, right? No (yawn), just the everyday life of working a Leveraged Sales business.

To protect yourself and your team, you need to know what these threats are and how to defend against them. Let's begin by defining the terms.

MLM ZOMBIES

They are the walking dead. They've been in so many deals that their credibility has long been deceased, but they keep lurking, looking for new uninformed victims. They determine which company to join based solely on their personal monetary upside, with absolutely no consideration about the viability of the product, the integrity of the people involved, or the legality of the deal. The only criteria that matters to them are the quality of the sweetheart deal they can negotiate and whether the concept can be readily marketed to exploit the gullible. The timing of when they jump from program to program is determined by how much time is remaining on their last sweetheart deal and whether someone else is offering them a better one.

About a decade ago, the company I was working with opened a new market and made one of these deals with a couple living here in the States. They rocketed up to the top income earner spot. During a forensic accounting audit, their undercover arrangement and a multitude of financial irregularities were uncovered. The CEO was fired, and the couple moved on to another program.

That couple jumped from one program to the next, to the next, to the next, joining at least four different ones in a year. The fired CEO promoted at least six or seven different programs within that same year. That sounds crazy, but here's what is even crazier. Both this couple and the CEO are still in the business, breathlessly promoting another hot deal every few months.

Unfortunately, these three people are not unique. There are probably another 15 or 20 zombie kings and queens still lumbering clumsily around the planet, eating the brains of everyone they encounter. Zombies never die.

The old-school model of MLM and network marketing is suffering from a zombie apocalypse right now. These zombies come into your company (usually with a sweetheart deal that includes an auto-qualified position or "cooked leg") and bring in lots of other zombies as well. The zombies rise through the comp plan rapidly and this impresses other lines. When the zombies rush to the next hot deal a few months later, they take some of these other people with them. This cycle repeats over and over, increasing the size of the zombie army for the next deal.

At the time I'm writing this, a lot of the U.S. and European markets have soured on the whole concept of buying leaders (known as "Business Development Agreements" or BDAs) and are strongly moving forward with the Leveraged Sales culture and model, leaving the zombies behind. However, in Australia and Asia, the zombies are still running amok, with a strong BDA culture still in place and people jumping from company to company.

Let's look at some ways to protect yourself and your team from these zombies. First of all, don't fall prey yourself. Don't think because you aren't successful yet, the cure is jumping into another program. If you divorce your spouse every time you have an argument, you're going to go through about 80 wedding rings and never experience a happy marriage. The chapter in *Direct Selling Success* on choosing the right company is the longest one in that book. Read it. And once you find the right company, stay with it through all of the trials and tribulations. If your company is successful, if there are other people who are succeeding in your company, then this means success in that company can be achieved—and it also means the reason for your lack of success is you, not the company.

Be extremely wary when zombies join your company. Don't be lulled into complacency because the zombies seem friendly and agreeable. They're only being nice to you now because they're thinking about how delicious your brains will taste when they start spooning them out of your skull.

If you're in an older, mature company, it probably has a pretty steady sales line, and it's not considered one of the "hot," trending companies. If a zombie comes into your company and starts popping rank advancement like the popcorn machine at the cinema, you're probably going to be tempted to edify and highlight their accomplishments to your own team and candidates—to show that hyper growth is still possible with your company. Don't. Do. This.

You can't edify a zombie's accomplishments without also edifying the zombie. This will always come back to haunt you. When they jump ship—and they will jump ship—you will suffer consequences if you have validated them and their activities in any way. The best strategy is to keep your team apart from the zombies and any events they do. (More about this later.)

DINOSAURS

Another threat to your team will come from the **dinosaurs**. These are the people metaphorically wearing MC Hammer parachute pants who think we're still living in the '90s. They may do as much damage to the business as the zombies do, because they're promoting in the sleazy, hype-y, and disingenuous style so common a few decades ago.

You'll know that you're dealing with a dinosaur because they follow the exact process taught in *Dinosaur MLM 101*. It looks a lot like this:

- They're gonna announce on social media that they're conducting intensive, unbiased research to discover the best opportunity available and solicit suggestions. (They don't even read what you send back; they're just collecting your contact info for the counter pitch.)

- They're gonna do a social media post about a huge announcement coming soon.

- They're gonna do a social media livestream where they say they have now found their "home." The broadcast will detail how they personally researched 437 companies to discover the only truly perfect opportunity ever to be developed since the earth's crust cooled. The breathless sensationalism will continue nonstop, suggesting that you won't ever need to sell products, go to training events, carry inventory, hold meetings, or recruit your friends and family.

- They're gonna do lots of Facebook posts (usually auto-posted every two hours) about how joyous it is to be able to work from their kitchen table, how many promotions they've had in their first seven days, how easy it is to help everyone succeed, and how the products that everyone wants just sell themselves. These will be alternated with snarky posts suggesting jobs are for "just over broke" losers, and only idiots attend college.

- They're gonna make reference to the "overwhelming number of people who have sent a DM" to unsettle you, even though nobody has.

- They're going to rent an exotic car for one hour and stage a social media photo shoot, trying to create the perception that the car is theirs.

- They're gonna post pix with, and share quotes from, other dinosaurs and parasites (see below), which they believe gives them industry cred.

The products or services of whatever company a dinosaur is representing are an afterthought. All dinosaurs design their presentations to center on bling-bling, money, and exotic supercars. When you go to their events, whether online or in person, you'll probably feel as if you've been magically (and tragically) transported back in time, to become an extra in a Flavor Flav video.

Dinosaurs create contrived urgency about timing and over-index on the comp plan. There's usually lots and lots of talk about hitting the exponential growth curve, momentum, and the next big thing. As I mentioned in Chapter 6, most of them have never experienced momentum and wouldn't have the slightest idea how to create it. But that doesn't stop them from hyping it. Keep something in mind...

There's only one thing worse than being in a company that never hits momentum. And that's being in a company *after* it has hit momentum.

If people are intoxicated with reaching momentum, they'll be the first to jump afterward, looking for the next "hot" company. So please don't make hitting momentum your primary recruiting benefit as the dinosaurs do. Look for a program that offers a great opportunity now, two years from now, and 10 years from now. And gear your presentations toward thinking people, not the ones who are impressed with hype and hysteria.

PARASITES

In nature (and Leveraged Sales), no organism lives its life in complete isolation. They have to interact with other organisms in some manner. In both the plant and the animal kingdom, there are many examples of **parasites** that either latch onto or infect a host. Since I'm guessing your new member orientation didn't include parasitology, and I'm sure you were lying awake last night wondering about the many different types of symbiotic relationships— allow me to conduct a brief science class on what you'll be facing in building your business.

Commensalism is a relationship where one species gains benefit and the other is unaffected. This type of parasite is rare because few hosts are unaffected by the symbionts. You won't see many relationships like these in Leveraged Sales.

Mutualism describes a relationship where both the host and symbiont benefit. You will happily experience many of these while working your business. There will be hotels that sell you meeting rooms, social media platforms on which you stream your presentations, and Lamborghini dealerships that sell your company all your bonus cars! You might engage a consultant or trainer to improve communication skills, learn proper etiquette, or better manage your finances. These are all mutually beneficial relationships.

Amensalism is a relationship between organisms of different species where one organism is unaffected, but the other one is impeded or destroyed. *These are the parasites you have to watch out for.*

There is an entire cottage industry of trainers, consultants, and coaches who create huge businesses by selling advice to us. A lot of them are former zombies or dinosaurs who have crashed out of the business. Many more such "experts" don't know the first thing about our profession, but they see a lucrative opportunity they can exploit. We have millions of distributors in our profession who are committed to lifetime learning, personal growth, and professional development—and are highly motivated to succeed. That makes many of us tempting targets.

These parasites claim to be astounding recruiters, brilliant sales coaches, or social media savants. Use a little common sense. If they really had the secret for success in our business, they'd be in the biz, killing it for themselves.

In the current business environment, you also have to inoculate your team against the review, watchdog, and industry news websites. The people who run these sites are experts at SEO marketing, so they always come up near the top of the results when people search company names. Ninety-five percent of these are detrimental to your business.

Some of these sites are well meaning but misguided. Some are designed solely as "bait and switch," meaning they lure you to read a review on your company, but it's actually a hit piece designed to switch you over to their company.

Some conduct polls for best trainer, CEO, or company. The real purpose of these surveys is to capture the emails of your team members so the parasites can either recruit them or sell them crap. Other sites employ "pay to play" models to determine who is featured. Don't allow yourself to be manipulated. These sites matter only to the zombies and dinosaurs who don't know any better. Stay away from them and keep your people off their mailing lists.

You also need to discern which blogs, newsletters, and magazines covering our profession actually provide value to build your business and aren't just a front to sell you shit. Many are just like the websites mentioned where people *buy* placement to be featured. The key word here is "discernment." Be discerning enough to know what kind of parasite you're dealing with.

TERRORISTS

Finally, we need to discuss the **terrorists.** The terrorists you'll face are the ones practicing criminal terrorism, using unethical tactics to commit crimes and reap undeserved profits. These people will do or say anything in their attempt to be successful. They fabricate outright lies in their recruiting efforts. They steal candidates from other people. They disparage and lie about you to your candidates. They manipulate orders or the back office to qualify for higher ranks. They will even attempt to steal distributors from their own team members.

Terrorists operate under situational ethics and can find a way to justify any behavior as long as there's some way they profit personally. They threaten not only the golden goose of their own company, but all the golden geese in the profession. When they're operating in your company, work to get them terminated. But you'll often find them in other companies. You have to fight against them there as well.

If you see a distributor from a competitor company crossing the line, report them to the legal department of their company. And if that doesn't solve the issue, report them to the appropriate government agency. If that seems radical to you, here's my belief. It hurts our profession less to report these people and get them shut down than it does to ignore them and allow them to destroy our reputation. When I saw outright pyramid schemes like Skybiz, BurnLounge, and OneCoin, I had no compunction about calling them out publicly. We need to police ourselves.

THIS IS NOT THE SAME THING AS COMPETING AGAINST A LEGITIMATE COMPETITOR

Every company has their own product line, comp plan, and support structure with both strengths and weaknesses. Your job is to make the best case for what you have to offer and present it in the most compelling way possible. The distributors in other companies also have a job to present what they have to offer in the most compelling way possible. If they do a better job than you do, tip your hat to them and resolve to do better next time. But never impugn the reputation of a legitimate competitor just because you're losing business to them. Instead of trying to tear them down, get better at what you do.

We've looked at some of the DEFCON 1 scenarios that might come from your team members, and now those that are created by people outside your company. But what about when the DEFCON 1 emergency is created by your own corporate team? Or because your company suddenly is gone? Those are the issues we'll explore next.

CHAPTER 9

Why 90 Percent of Current Companies Will Be Extinct by 2025

In 2017, I was about to update the fifth edition of my first book on network marketing when I suddenly had a better idea—to write an entirely new book, *Direct Selling Success*. I recognized we had undergone such cataclysmic and significant change in the profession, that the rules had altered completely. The regulatory environment, social media, technology, and e-commerce have changed the game forever. I reached the conclusion that we needed to leave the old business model to the dinosaurs and zombies and move into the future with the Leveraged Sales model.

At first I was a voice in the wilderness, because people thought I was an alarmist and overreacting. But month by month, as developments in the market and regulatory oversight played out, events have proven me right. Here's my next bold prediction:

Copy the 2020 list of the "DSN Global 100," the top 100 companies based on revenue compiled each year by *Direct Selling News* magazine. Save it and revisit it in 2026. *I will wager that at least 90 percent of the companies on the first list will be off the list by the end of 2025.* They will have changed their business model, been bought out, or be completely out of business.

That shocks a lot of people when I say it. But take a look back at what used to be the largest companies in the business world on the Standard and Poor Index, New York Stock Exchange, or other similar platforms around the world. There were companies like Kodak, Kresge, and General Motors. Companies that made it to these lists usually stayed on them for decades. But with the advent of technology, the relevance and life cycles of companies have accelerated to almost lightspeed levels.

If you check the 2010 list against the 2020 list, you'll see that the amount of change is mind-boggling. This wasn't true in the '50s, '60s and '70s. If you study the growth in value of companies like Apple, Google, and Amazon, they passed those companies that used to be considered veritable institutions like they were standing still. (Which is some sense, they were.)

I hate to say it, but the companies in our space are not as sophisticated as many of these former great companies that are now extinct. In fact, many are downright antediluvian. Direct Selling companies have been positively glacial in the speed with which they have adopted technology. Allow me to share the five reasons why 90 percent of these current companies will become extinct.

1) THEY DON'T HAVE A VIABLE PRODUCT LINE TO COMPETE

There are too many one-product companies. A product is a product; it's not a business model. Even if it's a hot, exciting, trendy, sexy, viral product. The hula hoop, pet rock, and frisbee were all sexy products. But a lasting business model requires a coherent product *line*.

There are too many product knockoffs in our space. In 2018 everybody came up with a keto diet product. Then in 2019 everyone came up with a CBD product. Even companies with completely unrelated product lines. We've lost the plot.

Companies succeed when they have a mission, a philosophy, and a reason for being beyond just earning profits. Your product line should be congruent with all that. Not a flavor-of-the-week mentality to keep up with the competition, or simply adding more products, regardless of fit, only because you have a distribution network. We have to get back to the fundamentals. The 5 percent of companies that survive the shakeout will have products that are:

- Unique
- Remarkable
- Exclusive
- Consumable

Even more importantly, the product line will add value, solve problems, or preferably do both. Most companies in our space are selling average-quality, generic products that are sold with different labels to multiple companies. If the product line for a company doesn't meet most or all of the criteria above, they won't last.

2) Their Business Model Can't Be Operated on a Smartphone

In the third world, people don't have laptops yet. In the first world, people have already moved on from laptops.

But everyone has smartphones and runs their lives on them.

All actions in the business—prospecting, ordering, enrolling, checking volume, communicating with your team, and all day-to-day requirements of the business— need to be functional from a cell phone. Mobile apps are vital for both prospecting and retailing. Companies that don't comply with this new reality quickly won't be able to compete.

3) THEY DON'T INVEST IN MARKETING INFRASTRUCTURE

If a company executive ever tells you, "These products just sell themselves," run away from them. Quickly.

Even heroin, crystal meth, and magic mushrooms needed some initial marketing. No matter how incredible your multivitamin, skin care line, or diet shakes are, nobody will ever know of them without marketing. That's what you get paid bonuses for—to market. And for you to do so effectively, you're going to need a marketing infrastructure in place, one provided by the company.

Not every company understands this. Some don't actually understand how the business works. Others think they can get away with a lower start-up investment by fobbing off all marketing functions and materials to the field. In both cases they are wrong, and such shortsightedness not only produces poor results but increases the likelihood of running into regulatory trouble. Trouble serious enough to get the whole operation shut down.

Let's start with the effectiveness issue. An effective marketing infrastructure today requires a seamless integration of both physical and digital resources. The digital elements include the corporate website, individual replicated websites for distributors, mobile apps, and voice assistants. The physical elements include items like flipcharts, professionally produced video presentations, brochures, and product catalogs.

These are not the kind of resources the average distributor is going to be able to develop. And let's be honest: Even if they can produce them, they'll never bring about duplication. *In order for these elements to be scalable and cost-effective, they need to be developed and produced by the corporate team.*

Perhaps the most important consideration in all this is the content of the marketing materials themselves. Your marketing materials must detail the benefits of the products, augmented by testimonials, case studies, and research. Explain the rewards of the compensation plan and the various award trips, car programs, and other incentives. Show the growth potential of the business and the rewards of being an independent distributor. If you leave the scripting of these messages to part-time distributors in the field, you are begging to be closed down by the regulators. And they'll be happy to oblige.

4) Their Comp Plan Sabotages the Results

Comp plan design is a very complex science. At the root of the science is creating a pay and reward structure that produces optimal behavior by the people participating in the plan. The field will quickly learn the best ways to maximize their payout from the plan. That's what they're supposed to do. You must have a plan that rewards them for taking the right actions and restricts their earning potential when they take actions that aren't for the highest good of their team. I would categorize the destructive plans in the following three buckets.

Bucket One: Poster Child Plans

You'll find these in the companies still pandering to the dinosaurs. Dinosaurs believe the secret of growing a company is to design a top-heavy plan to the get one or two "poster boys" (or "poster girls") to an income of 100K in dollars or euros per month as quickly as possible. Then they kick in the hype and rah-rah machine, using the poster child as bait to lure in others who think this kind of success is possible for them as well. In actuality, that result is *not* possible for everyone. These plans have a huge churn ratio, with most people burning out eventually. Companies with these plans will be forced to change or they'll be eliminated.

Bucket Two: "CEO Couldn't Buy a Clue About the Business" Plans

Comp plan design requires tremendous sophistication. Not every president or CEO has a sophisticated understanding of how the business works in the field. When their company hits a sales plateau, they sometimes react with a blunt-instrument mentality. For example, they might think, "These leaders make so much money and they don't work hard enough. Let's change the Diamond Director qualifying criterion from 200,000 points to 400,000." The end result is just a lot of leaders feeling betrayed and not qualifying at rank. They become demoralized and start shopping around for somewhere else to work.

Or the executive unwittingly thinks, "The problem is the field isn't enrolling enough new people. I'm going to change the rank qualification rules for leaders, so they have to personally sponsor 10 new distributors every month." In their mind, it sounds good, looks good, even looks good on paper. In reality, it's a terrible idea....

Because once a leader has a large group (10,000+ team members), their highest good to both their team and the company is *not* to be recruiting 10 new distributors a month. They would be so busy holding the hands of these 10 new people each month—conducting their first presentations with them, reassuring them, guiding them through their initial training—that they wouldn't have time to handle important team functions like event agendas, team communications, recruiting presentations, and other actions that can affect thousands or tens of thousands of distributors. Field leaders grow companies. Field leaders who have to spend a disproportionate percentage of their time making sure they are still qualified don't grow companies. They plateau or shrink them.

Bucket Three: Plans That Penalize Retailers

If you analyze the comp plans of 100 different companies, it's a pretty good bet that 90 of the companies don't give the same level and quality of compensation to retailers as they offer recruiters. Look at your qualifications for award trips, bonus cars, and bonus pools. Do they require a certain number of distributor enrollments in order to achieve them? If so, the message you are sending is that retailers aren't important to you. (I would wager that in the majority of companies today, there actually is not a path for retailers to earn a bonus car or many award trips.)

Team members always build according to the plan rewards. If your plan doesn't reward retailing activities equal to recruiting activities, you're sending a subconscious message (and constructing a culture) to focus on recruiting at the expense of developing a customer base. The companies that do this will end up in regulatory trouble and are likely to be closed down.

5) THEY HAVEN'T BECOME TECH COMPANIES

In my last book I challenged all Leveraged Sales companies to become tech companies first and foremost. Instead of thinking like a skin care company, think about how Apple would sell skin care. Instead of thinking like a wellness company, think how Amazon sells wellness products. The two areas in which most companies are seriously deficient—from a technology standpoint—are e-commerce and social media.

Social Media Failures

Let's begin with the lesser: social media. For a company, your social media presence helps create your brand, allows you to communicate with customers, and bolsters your ability to build confidence and connection with your distributors. Most companies today have a low-level intern handling all their social media accounts. And it shows. The posts they're putting out are usually just poor attempts at advertising. But the biggest danger of this ignorance on social media comes from the fact that the company has no policies, procedures, or training for the distributors on how to use social media. As a result, one of two scenarios plays out:

1. The distributors don't employ social media, making them uncompetitive in the market.

2. The distributors make it up as they go along, posting outlandish product claims or income testimonials that serve as flashing targets to the regulators.

E-Commerce Failures

But the main area in which Leveraged Sales companies have fallen behind—and I mean light-years behind—is e-commerce.

There is no bigger migration of customers anywhere in the world—from one platform to another—than the current multitude of people who have moved (and are moving) from buying through conventional methods into shopping through e-commerce.

Yet the companies in our field are woefully unprepared, inadequate, and frankly, incompetent. Today we have companies creating rules against marketing on sites like Shopify, eBay, and Alibaba, fiercely fighting the inevitable. This will end no differently than it did for the record companies who fought streaming music, the catalog companies that fought the department stores, and the department stores that fought the Internet.

The companies in Leveraged Sales have to integrate capacity for all distributors to market their products and services through e-commerce. And not just in insignificant, add-on ways. Each company needs a robust model of process, training, and support in e-commerce. A distributor should have the ability to operate their entire business through an e-commerce model should they choose to. And the companies that don't facilitate this change will go the way of record stores, travel agents, and neighborhood Blockbuster Video outlets.

Now you've seen the five main reasons most companies in our space are going to become extinct within five years. What if your company is lacking in these areas? Lend this book to your company execs and ask them to read this chapter. You're going to have to use all the influence you have to try and convince them of the importance of these five tripwires. Because if they don't understand the magnitude of the situation, you're going to be faced with a very difficult dilemma.

If your company has these five areas handled, congratulations. This means at least they're not automatically guaranteed to be dinosaurs by the end of 2025. But you're not out of the woods yet...

Because companies also take stupid, negligent, or even illegal actions that can produce DEFCON 1 crises. And sometimes it's because you have a brilliant, visionary founder—who just might unconsciously destroy the company they love. In the next chapter, we'll study how to know if you're in danger of that—and what to do if you are.

CHAPTER 10

Why Brilliant, Visionary CEOs and Founders Usually Fail

Steve Jobs was a brilliant visionary who made Apple one of the most valuable companies in the world. But that would have never happened were he not first fired from the company. (It was only many years later, when he was much wiser and able to learn from his first disaster as a founder, that he was able to bring value to the company and its customers.) Today, Uber is another one of the most valuable companies in the world. And which also unceremoniously dumped their founder. Literally the week I am writing this chapter, the company WeWork, which recently launched their IPO, paid a $1.7 billion (with a "B") golden parachute to make their founder go away.

I hate to affirm a negative outcome into existence. But I'm afraid it's probable that what I write in this chapter and the next are going to cost me a lot of book sales. Because the people who inspire me to write these chapters may want to ban the book from their companies.

But I would be remiss if I didn't cover this topic. Because sometimes—sadly, far too often—the toxic, dysfunctional person at your company is the one who created it. Or the biggest obstacles to success with the company are the people who run it. And you deserve to know the truth.

Here's something very simple yet very profound that you must understand. The skillsets (and personality type) it takes to launch a company are dramatically different from the skillsets (and personality type) it takes to manage a company. As they say Down Under, it's chalk and cheese.

BOLD VISION DOES NOT EQUAL GOOD MANAGEMENT

If I could distill one misconception charismatic founders have, and one that kills them the most, it's their belief they can somehow avoid making unpopular decisions. Let's start with a foundational premise: To add value, you must sometimes make unpopular decisions. Because if the decisions you make are always popular, then you aren't actually adding any value.

Founders, presidents, and CEOs (at least good ones) are required to make difficult decisions like firing people, closing down an unprofitable or unsuccessful product or division, and laying off people. But many dynamic, charismatic founders aren't ready for this. They've grown accustomed to commanding respect, basking in admiration, and luxuriating in their popularity. Often this translates into dysfunctional behavior, such as the inability to terminate incompetent people. They just keep moving them around from job to job, where ultimately they leave a trail of chaos, confusion, and calamity in their wake.

Founder personality types live off the high of launching new ventures, creating bold visions, and inspiring others to follow them. They despise being bothered with those annoying realities like human resources, finances, and logistics. The best way I know to demonstrate this is with another embarrassing confession: I'm the perfect case study of this reality.

When I launched my speaking and training business, it became an immediate success. I flew around the world conducting public seminars for thousands of attendees. Companies practically threw money at me to develop training programs and materials for their teams. My own company sales kept going up and up, and I kept hiring more employees to keep the home office operating while I hopscotched around the globe. I ran the company from my shirt pocket and phone booths. (Google it.) My market share kept expanding, my books and training albums were selling like hotcakes, and I pretty much became the go-to, definitive expert in the space. There was only one problem with all of that success. I wasn't making any actual, you know, money. I kept driving harder, thinking that I could eventually get the sales so high that they would outrun the expenses. But they never did.

Because as I reluctantly came to understand, I was a brilliant leader. And a terrible manager.

Finally, I realized I needed to hire a dynamic CEO or VP of operations to run the day-to-day management of the business—and allow me to continue my role as the rainmaker bringing in the money. I advertised the position and narrowed the interview list down to six candidates.

At the very first interview, I was blown away by the candidate. She had been the executive assistant to Frank

Borman, the former astronaut who went on to run Eastern Airlines, at that time the largest carrier in the world. I wanted to give her the job on the spot. But I had those other five people already scheduled...

I went through the process of talking to everyone but remained convinced that the first candidate was the right person for the job. Until I got to the sixth interview with a woman named Sherry Peacock. The interview was being conducted in my office, with my desk submerged by stacks of papers and folders, surrounded with stacks and stacks of other file folders strewn around the floor.

About 20 minutes into the interview, Sherry leaned forward and in a very matter of fact tone said, "I need to let you know something. If you decide to hire me, you're going to have to meet me here one Saturday morning, and we're going to sort through and organize all these stacks of papers and folders. And if you don't, I will wait until you fly out on one of your trips, and I'll just throw them all away."

I hired her on the spot.

I hired her to be my boss. To run the company, deciding all of the things like salaries and raises, vacation time and sick days, scheduling, bookkeeping, paying bills, and all of the other necessities of keeping a business running. That allowed me to play to my strengths, and we were back in profit within a few months. Sherry ran the whole operation for me until I sold the company. And I still have my own version of Pepper Potts, a lady named Lornette who has been keeping me out of the ditches for the last 25 years.

I tell this story to company founders and executives all the time, hoping they will learn from my mistakes.

(It's entirely possible that the most important return on investment you'll get from this book is by kidnapping your founder, tying them to a chair, and reading this chapter aloud to them.)

Unfortunately, this story in and of itself may not be enough to penetrate the delusion and denial of your founder. It's usually not enough when I tell it to my consulting clients either. There are not many people with the emotional maturity, humility, and wisdom who can be a visionary founder, but also recognize that they need to fire themselves at some point and bring in a team to make the trains run on time. Because there are so many dynamics at play here.

Certainly, ego is one. For years I've been arguing that ego doesn't have to be a bad thing. It requires a strong, healthy ego to have the guts to launch a company. (The meek might inherit the earth, but they don't usually create successful new companies.) You have to believe in your dream when almost no one else in the world does. You have to face rejection, doubt, criticism, and even ridicule. You have to be strong enough in your vision to sell that vision to investors, partners, employees, team members, and even vendors. Elon Musk once compared being a founder to eating glass while staring into the abyss of death.

Founders are immune to rejection, doubt, criticism, ridicule, and eating glass. They are such powerful people that they have the balls or feminine grit to power forward, no matter the external doubts, critics, and haters. They're a rare breed, and one that the world desperately needs. But when their ego is so over-inflated that they can't see how they are inhibiting growth and progress, company failure is frequently the result.

Often the inherent flaw isn't ego, but the unwillingness to give up control. You see this a lot with science- and nutrition-based companies. The founder might be a brilliant scientist or researcher who develops a breakthrough product. They're quite literally a genius in their area of expertise. But they know nothing about logistics, HR, finances, IT, and the multitude of other necessary workings of operating a company. They believe their invention or development is so powerful, it's not only going to sell itself, but sell so many units that having competent management or not doesn't matter. They attempt to control everything and tune out anyone who doesn't drink the Kool-Aid. In their desperate attempt to protect "their baby," they end up killing it.

Founders don't have to be scientists for this to happen. Sometimes they're simply a brilliant entrepreneur with a product concept that disrupts an industry (like the Uber and WeWork founders), and they can't understand that the entrepreneurial skills that made them perfect candidates to birth the idea are the very same traits that kill management, organization, and logistics. Often, they are wildly charismatic, and people naturally want to follow them. But this innate magnetism won't prevent the failure that is inevitable.

THE MARTYR LEADER

All of these scenarios highlight similar symptoms. The leader can't properly delegate responsibilities, everyone reports to them, and they hire incompetent sycophants or family members. *In other words, they surround themselves with enablers.* They are the locus of the company—the lonely martyr—always putting out fires, because they don't trust enough to hire competent people and let them do their job. This means the executives they have in place need to bring everything back to the martyr for approval. Or worse, these executives turn everything they touch into a train wreck, dumpster fire, or shitshow. And then the martyr has to swoop in and save the day.

The leader then points to these experiences as evidence that they alone can handle the important issues—and uses them to justify why they can't delegate responsibly. Eventually, the martyr becomes a full-time firefighter in charge of dumpster fires and no longer has time to unleash the mad genius talent that they actually possess.

Every new start-up company will sort through issues like who reports to whom and what the job requirements for each position are. And early on, all employees will need to perform extra tasks. That's normal for a young, developing company. But what you see when a founder doesn't understand operations are not the growing pains of a new venture. It is a frenzied, chaotic, and dangerous mess that prevents the company from becoming successful.

Every employee in a company should have one person they report to. When you have a martyr leader, everyone has two people—the one they're told is their boss and then their real boss (the martyr leader). This disrupts the chain of command, undercuts the ability of the person who is supposed to be reported to, and guarantees dysfunction.

Since the martyr leader must control everything, the executives reporting to them don't really have clearly defined roles and responsibilities. Their job entails reacting to whatever crisis is consuming the martyr in the moment. So an average week for the executive (let's say she's a vice president of sales) might be renting an arena for the company convention, submitting product formulas for approval in a future country to open, hiring the new janitor, creating a PowerPoint for the martyr's next meeting, ordering office supplies, speaking to the teacher or guidance counselor of the martyr's child, scheduling a board of directors meeting, posting on the martyr's Twitter account, negotiating credit extensions with vendors, and ordering a cemetery plot for the martyr. Seriously.

These executives can't possibly succeed, even if they were competent (which they're usually not). Some of these tasks, like submitting products for approval in a new country, require extensive local knowledge of the languages, laws, and customs. Likewise with renting the right venue and planning a convention. You need people who are trained in these areas. When this doesn't happen, the results can be disastrous. Frequently, the founder doesn't have an understanding of what a CFO, head of HR, CTO, or COO actually does in the course of their responsibilities. (One founder I know ran out of funds and was absolutely convinced that his people had stolen millions of dollars. The actual situation was that the company's sales had grown so fast, it required $7 million in product inventory on hand.)

If your visionary leader is open to change but not sure how to do it, give them this chapter. Additionally, some helpful and instructive books for them to read are:

- *The Hard Thing About Hard Things* by Ben Horowitz

- *What You Do Is Who You Are: How to Create Your Business Culture* by Ben Horowitz (Also a good read for top field leaders.)
- *High Output Management* by Andy Grove
- *It Worked for Me: In Life and Leadership* by Colin Powell

As I said, many of these leaders are charismatic and really are genius while swimming in their proper lane. But that won't stop them from unwittingly destroying their own companies. And if you and your team are in their company, you will become the collateral damage. Before you jump on board a company simply because they have a brilliant, charming founder, think it all the way through. If they fit this profile, they will ultimately create a DEF-CON 1 situation for you. Do your due diligence on all of the other important considerations.

In the earlier chapters we looked at the partnership necessary between the field and corporate. But sometimes you'll run into management that doesn't buy into that. They're autocrats and think they can just demand compliance with whatever policies and procedures they come up with. Other times they mean well, but they don't have a competent team assembled in the HQ. And sadly, yet other times, you discover that they simply are not people of integrity. That's what we will explore next.

CHAPTER 11

Dealing with Corporate Mistakes, Incompetence, or Malfeasance

When we choose to work with a company, we know there will be serious consequences, both wonderful and horrific. Most of the people who join our space don't have the necessary experience and insights to know how to select the right company for them. It's why the chapter on selecting the right company in *Direct Selling Success* tops out at more than 5,000 words. That book, and especially that chapter, are making a sea change in our profession already, because they give people tools to make that decision with confidence and accuracy. Because of that book, there's no need to repeat company selection material here. But what we must cover in this field manual for leaders are the risks and rewards, the hard realities of starting and running a business that leave you vulnerable and dependent on another partner—in this case the company.

Let's look at some of the specific DEFCON 1 situations your company might create for you and how you can best respond to protect you and your team.

THE COMPANY EMPLOYS INCOMPETENT PEOPLE IN IMPORTANT POSITIONS

Let me share an actual example. I was working with a company slated to open the Spain market in December that year. My field leaders and I had many contacts there and knew the opening date about eight months ahead of time, so we had been doing extensive prelaunch work. We had six experienced leaders ready to go and about 60 additional people ready to enroll and order as soon as the back office went live. In November the company moved the launch to January. In December they bumped it back to February. I started applying serious pressure, explaining how we were all losing credibility and in danger of the potential team members going somewhere else. To prevent yet another black eye, in January the company moved the opening way back to mid-April. By April 1 it was obvious we were nowhere close. I went ballistic, demanding a meeting with the president/founder.

He was a textbook martyr leader like you read about in Chapter 10, running everything spur of the moment, rushing from one disaster to the next. The person he put in charge of international expansion was a lawyer. Let's call him Frank. Frank came to the job with no training or experience in the business or opening markets. While a nice guy who worked hard and absolutely meant well, Frank was completely incompetent in the job he was being asked to perform. The martyr leader announced that he would host a video meeting with Frank, myself, and two other top field leaders every Tuesday morning until the market was open.

Sure enough, the following Tuesday we had our first meeting and Frank announced that Spain was opening in four weeks. I wanted to know if we had an office yet. No. Did we have a GM or country manager? No. Was the website translated for Catalan? No. Was the product registration for the government complete? No. I pointed out that if the translation and registration were not complete, then the products couldn't even be in production yet. They weren't. I pointed out how absolutely preposterous it was to think that we would be open in four weeks. Although somewhat sheepish, Frank declared that he had faced similar situations in other countries and got them all opened. (I later learned that all these previous openings had also been months or even years behind schedule.) For the next three weeks, Frank kept insisting that the deadline would be met and the market opened as promised. The other leaders and I were no longer stupid enough to relay these preposterous promises to the potential recruits, and they steadily dropped away to join other companies.

On opening week, we had another meeting in which Frank insisted that we would open the following week. I demanded an update on the necessary steps: office rented, GM hired, website translated, etc. Still, at least 90 percent of it wasn't done. I couldn't hold back any longer. I announced that only an insane person could believe we would be open in a week, demanded they send Frank for a psychological checkup, then left the video meeting.

About five minutes later, I received a call from the major investor who had also been in the meeting. He said

Frank was offended, scolded me for joking that Frank was insane, and suggested I should apologize. I explained that I wasn't joking, I literally thought Frank was crazy. And then I suggested that if the investor didn't also think Frank was insane, he was probably insane himself.

That didn't go over well.

This acrimonious relationship continued for months. There was a huge contingent of employees inside the corporate headquarters sticking pins in Randy Gage voodoo dolls every day. (Although I was a folk hero to those employees who actually cared about fixing the dysfunctional culture.) But being wildly unpopular was a price I was willing to pay—*and you have to be willing to pay*—to give your team their best chance of survival when faced with situations like these.

THE COMPANY KEEPS OVERPROMISING ON RELEASES (NEW PRODUCTS, MARKETING MATERIALS, OR PROMOTIONS) AT MAJOR EVENTS AND THEN DOESN'T DELIVER ON TIME

This situation is similar to the one above. For whatever reason, the word of the company is no good. It could be incompetence, sloppy accountability, or delusional expectations. It almost doesn't matter what the cause is. What does matter is that the company has no credibility and if you simply parrot their broken promises, you and your other leaders will lose credibility as well. If this happens, you will no longer be able to lead and grow the team effectively. In situations like this it may be necessary to "Big Foot" (throw your weight around as a top distributor) the company, exerting maximum pressure.

Every time the company blows another release, you're going to need to force them to conduct "system versus outcome" decision analysis after the fact. It's vitally necessary to discover the inherent flaws in the company's decisions that are creating the negative outcomes. Example: How are the people who make these decisions selected? Who hires them and who do they report to? How are they rewarded? Do they get paid on promotion, actual results, or actual sales? Did that reward structure impact their decision? (And to answer your question: No, of course it's not your job to do this. Doing this isn't even within the postal code of your responsibilities as a distributor. But when the situation gets to DEFCON 1 level, you do whatever is required to protect your team.)

In the event that the company doesn't correct its behavior, you may need to disavow their conduct and train your team along a very unconventional track. Example: When the company announces a launch, you would tell your people something like, "We won't be promoting this launch to our team members. We will wait until the product actually comes out, and only then will we start to include it into our presentations."

Make no mistake: This is a horrible way to operate. It also happens to be less horrible than not doing it. Because if you keep enabling a company that misses most deadlines, you'll end up losing your team. Better to operate in a less-than-desirable environment but stay in business. If that still doesn't fix the situation, you'll have to consider a final solution. (More about that in the following chapter.)

THE COMPANY PROMOTES CRAPPY OR OFF-SYSTEM MARKETING MATERIALS TO THE NETWORK

Same as above:

1. Big Foot
2. Unplug from the company, if necessary, to save the team.
3. If that still doesn't fix the situation, you'll have to consider a final solution. (More about that in the next chapter.)

THE COMPANY IS PARALYZED BY INTERNAL POLITICS

Same as above:

1. Big Foot
2. Unplug from the company, if necessary, to save the team.
3. If that still doesn't fix the situation, you'll have to consider a final solution. (More about that in the next chapter.)

THE COMP PLAN ISN'T WORKING, OR THE COMPANY MAKES CHANGES THAT BACKFIRE

Comp plan changes are one of the most dangerous actions a company can take. They are frequently the cause of a company collapsing. Even when the change is well planned and improves the overall situation, *any* modification is still fraught with danger. Be mindful that there is a finite amount of money that goes into the plan. For the sake of the example, let's suppose 50 percent of the sales volume is contributed to the plan. Every single change you make in how that money is distributed has both a winner and a loser. So even when the change is positive, well intentioned, and actually produces the right effect—meaning the company and field are both stronger and the correct behavior is being rewarded—there will still always be someone who was being rewarded for incorrect behavior. And, news flash, they are not going to be happy with the change. People *hate* when you mess with their money.

About 15 years ago I was with a company that made a change to the comp plan. It was a good and necessary change and worked out surprisingly well. But one guy in Atlanta, who usually earned about $300 monthly on a part-time basis, lost approximately $11 a month from his check with the new plan. He went on a crusade to destroy the company, creating an "ABC Company Sucks" website, posting in public forums, making complaints to regulators, calling TV stations, and so on. He saw himself as a gallant hero, fighting the forces of evil. Of course, he destroyed the little residual income he had developed and eventually dropped out and moved on to save the world from another grievous injustice. But he was a complete pain-in-the-ass distraction for four months or so.

What you have to protect against is a kneejerk reaction to comp plan changes. The default setting is always "This totally sucks! The company changed the plan so they and their favorite distributors at the top can get more money for themselves." Sometimes that is actually true. Usually, it's not. Much as the company is the golden goose for the field, the field is the golden goose for the company. Most companies are not foolish enough to intentionally alienate their field leadership team. More often these mistakes come about because a company has either miscalculated or received bad advice.

You have to be a big kid and a critical thinker; mature enough not just to fight for more money for yourself and the team. If the company isn't financially viable, the golden goose dies. The company needs to meet all of its expenses, have money for research and development, be able to fund future expansion, and produce a reward for the shareholders. You have to support all those objectives, not just the ones that boost your own bonus check.

At least five times in my career, I have been on an advisory board or committee that worked with the company on a comp plan change where I personally agreed to changes that reduced my commissions for the short term. When I was earning $140,000 a month, I helped enact a change that knocked $20,000 off that. Once, with a new company opening in my country for the first time, I asked the general manager to remove me from a bonus pool so the remaining shares would be worth more for my emerging leaders. I didn't do these actions because I'm a philanthropist (although I am one), but because I felt that ultimately the company and my team would be healthier and produce more growth if we reallocated more money to the middle of the plan. (This is where people were just starting to enter the leadership ranks and would be needing to buy plane tickets and make other investments in growing their own teams.)

Avoid a DEFCON 1 Meltdown

If you want to avoid a DEFCON 1 meltdown where the company blows up, be willing to sacrifice personally making the absolute most amount of money you can and think of the greater good of your team.

If you're a top leader, comp plan changes and design are definitely cases when you should Big Foot it. Promulgate the concept of the company running parallel comp plans for at least six months. This means the company actually runs two simultaneous commission plans, the old and the new, each pay period. The distributor gets paid whichever version is higher on a steady declining percentage each month. (Companies: I don't want to get lost in the weeds on the fine points of this here, so call me for consulting if you're in this situation.) All the distributors will get to see what they earn in each plan, so they can learn exactly what behavior they need to change in order to maximize their payout with the new plan before the final switchover happens.

A Modification That Needs to Play out in a Lot of Existing Companies

As I mentioned in Chapter 9, many company comp plans are skewed to recruiting, not customer acquisition. These companies will need to make changes to reward retailers if they want to survive. So, for example, maybe now someone earns a free bonus car if they produce a group volume of 10,000 points a month. The plan might need to change so the free car is awarded only if they both produce 10,000 points a month *and have 10 retail customers on autoship*. If you just implement that change overnight, you're going to have a lot of pissed-off people who are not qualifying at rank. But if the new policy is phased in over a period of months, people can see exactly what they have to change in order to get the best bonus check they can earn.

The Most Important Part

Before you change a comp plan, you make many trial runs to see how the payout will change. Understand that trial runs are not simulations. There is no way to run an actual simulation, because there's no way to predict human behavior. Like in a scientific experiment, each comp plan change is a hypothesis, one that must be tested and proven. And the only way to do that is to put the plan in action and see what happens when actual human behavior and buying habits play out.

As you and the company traverse along this six- or eight-month runway, you will see how the payouts change and whether or not they are producing the desired effects. You might discover that the new plan blows up the cap and would bankrupt the company. Or you might discover that the plan can be gamed, so people exploit the flaw, resulting in undesired behavior. You could even determine that the planned changes produce too much breakage for the company and cause the bonus checks to nosedive. If you have insisted that a committee of field leaders be involved with the process, the group can partner with the company to make necessary modifications before the damage becomes fatal. A lot of pain and heartbreak can be alleviated this way.

As with most potential DEFCON 1 situations, *the best response is to inoculate the field ahead of time.* Let them know of upcoming changes from the field leadership. Announce the coming changes, help the team prepare for them, and explain why the modifications will ultimately be good, even if there are negative short-term consequences. Don't let the team learn of a change from a company email or a complaint made by someone crossline. Be proactive and partner with the company. If they won't cooperate, I'll detail how to handle that in the next chapter.

The Executives Are Totally out of Touch with What Happens in the Field—Yet Convinced They're Omniscient, Omnipotent Geniuses

Company executives who don't understand what happens in the field are dangerous to everybody, themselves included. They make bad decisions, which have disastrous consequences.

An example of how this might play out is when they design criteria for contests and promotions. Almost 20 years ago I was working with a company where the VP of marketing loved going on cruises. Naturally, he always created contests for the field that awarded seven- or 10-day cruises for high achievers. And he was working with a budget, so he shopped around to get the best deals. For whatever reason, the best deals usually ended up on cruises that were at sea during the time one month ended and another began. This meant nothing to him; a great deal was a great deal.

To me, this was an unmitigated disaster. Think about it. At that time, on a cruise ship at sea, the passengers were pretty much cut off from the world. No one had iPhones or cell service. A few ships had Internet, but you had to go to a special room in the bowels of the ship and pay about $10 a minute just to check your email. And my company had a monthly pay plan.

What do you think happened to sales and new rank advancements when my very best people were out to sea—figuratively and literally—essentially incommunicado when the month ended?

In this case, the executive wasn't an arrogant person, but actually a great guy to work with overall. But being in the corporate HQ instead of the field, he wasn't aware of the many important actions that field leaders implement each pay period to close out strong.

All companies make mistakes, just like all field leaders make mistakes. The big issue comes when the company can't acknowledge their mistakes or are so arrogant they think they know field activities better than the field does. They might think the products are so magical that they market themselves, or they just simply don't understand the process that brings in customers and distributors.

Remember "Frank" from the disaster in Spain story above? The guy who lied about the opening date every week for more than a year and conducted a clinic on how to break promises and miss deadlines? A few months after that, the company asked him to speak at the leadership conference for top earners. Can you guess what he chose as a topic?

Keeping Your Word.

You can't make this shit up. I swear on all that is holy, that is the actual topic he selected to share. He stood at the front of the room lecturing us for 45 minutes, using PowerPoint slides like "Your Word Is Your Bond," "Speak with Integrity," and "Be Accountable." Every leader in the room was positively gobsmacked. Incredulous WhatsApp messages were flying back and forth, but he droned on, completely oblivious to the irony of the situation.

Another company I worked with, when planning its first annual convention, arranged the entire agenda without any input from the field. There were keynote speeches from the president, CEO, CFO, customer service manager, distributor services manager, VP marketing, VP sales, VP production, and VP of some department nobody's ever heard of. (Every single one of these speakers was a white man.)

What we learned from this experience is that every company executive secretly desires to be an inspirational keynote speaker.

Not one of these speakers spoke about their area of expertise and how it could benefit the distributors. Not one of them provided any actionable training on how to work the business more effectively. They all presented material stolen from motivational speakers they'd heard over the years. And these obviously had not been good motivational speakers.

So for two days straight we heard stale, antediluvian speeches about putting on your own oxygen mask first in the airplane, why mama eagles push the baby eagles out of the nest, the Roger Bannister four-minute mile story, and the god-forsaken starfish story. ("It made a difference to that one.") Kill me now.

If you're a company executive reading this, let me provide you with a clue....

The only time your CFO should be giving a speech is when they're attending a convention of accountants. There is no other forum on earth where people want to hear a speech from a CFO. (Other than your local fire department, when they need to clear a room fast.) In the course of those two days, 1,000 new distributors went from eager and inspired to despondent and comatose. But here's the worst part: The distributors didn't learn any business-building techniques, they didn't hear any success stories from the field to build belief, and—unless they were a middle-aged white guy—they didn't hear from anyone that looked like them or their team.

In this situation, the company actually meant well. They had invested a huge amount of time and money on the event. Like many of the zombies and dinosaurs in the field, they didn't understand that events have to contain more than feel-good rah-rah.

Every event involves taking your best, most active people out of the field for several days or more. It's a huge deal for those people to arrange time off work, make arrangements for children and pets, and invest money on airfare, accommodations, and meals.

When You Schedule an Event, Have an Objective for It

After this convention, my sponsor, several other top leaders, and I met with the CEO and explained all of this. And we made clear that if the company didn't consult with us on future agendas, we would schedule our own conventions and instruct our people not to attend the corporate events. (Fortunately, they agreed and a productive partnership was created.) You have to do the same.

THE COMPANY BECOMES THE TARGET OF REGULATORY ACTION OR NEGATIVE PUBLICITY

If you're the target of the first, you will also become the target of the second. Sometimes it isn't regulators causing grief but the negative attention of a media outlet. In cases like this—and pretty much any crisis or DEFCON 1 scenario—one piece of advice will always serve you well:

Calm Is Contagious

If you panic, you can guarantee your team will be hysterical and expect worst-case outcomes. If you're calm, the team will respond a lot more favorably. Don't allow yourself to be drawn into fright and terror mode. Airlines have planes that crash, killing hundreds of passengers—yet they survive. Public companies have leaders embroiled in sex scandals—yet they recover. Restaurant chains have patrons die of food poisoning—yet they rebound.

Just because you're receiving negative publicity doesn't mean it is warranted. And just because regulators are attacking you doesn't guarantee they're right. Sometimes you're the victim of misrepresentation. And sometimes your company has made a mistake. Either case doesn't have to be fatal.

The public is remarkably forgiving if they feel you made an honest mistake, you're genuinely sorry, and you're committed to making sure it doesn't happen again.

(And so are your team members.) In the case of crisis situations, here are the best ways to respond.

- *Be calm. State the facts. Be honest.* Example: "We have received word that the Texas Attorney General is filing a restraining order against the company alleging deceptive recruiting practices. We're committed to making sure all of our associates conduct themselves morally, ethically, and legally. We are investigating the source of their complaints and cooperating with the government completely. Our executive team and legal department are working with the investigators to find a resolution that works for everyone involved. We'll get to the bottom of this and will keep you updated along the way."

- *Control the narrative.* Be the first to bring up issues to your customers and team members. Make sure they hear about the problem from you first, not in a *Breaking News Alert* on their phones. Get your side of the story out before the other side sets the narrative. If you inoculate the field by bringing any problems to them first, they're much more likely to remain composed and support the company as things are worked out.

- *Maintain regular updates.* If you and the company go radio silent, rumors and gossip will run rampant. Keep everyone apprised of the situation along the way.

- *If you mess up, own up.* Example: "We've been advised that a batch of the strawberry-flavor protein shake may have been contaminated and created adverse side effects for some people who consumed it. Effective immediately, we are recalling all shakes with batch number 123456. Please destroy any inventory you have. We have already issued credits to everyone who purchased this product. Our foremost concern is the people affected, and we're doing everything we can to support their treatment, discover how this happened, and put safeguards in place to ensure it never happens again. If you have any questions or concerns, we've set up a hotline at 1-800-XXX-XXXX to serve you."

Companies survive some of the most dangerous crisis situations. But only if the corporate team and the field leadership work together to stay calm, keep communication lines open, and demonstrate their commitment to making things right.

COMPANY EXECS ARE ABUSING THEIR LEADERSHIP POSITIONS

If someone from the corporate team (or field leadership) is:

- Bullying someone
- Showing favoritism to certain lines or withholding support from others
- Encouraging unethical behavior like line switches
- Having an affair with someone in the team
- Making deals to financially participate in distributorships

...that person should be reported to the company immediately. In the case of dangerous and illegal activity like sexual assault, rape, molesting a child, or threatening behavior, first notify the police. Then follow up immediately to alert the company of the situation.

Your primary responsibility is to protect your team. They must know they are safe from abuse of leadership in any capacity. If you report such activity to the company and it isn't addressed—or if that activity comes from the highest levels of leadership and there is no one above them to address it—you'll need to consider the final solutions outlined in the next chapter.

THE COMPANY IS MAKING BAD DEALS WITH ZOMBIES AND DINOSAURS

Building a large successful company with strong field leadership is extremely tough and takes a long time. But that will never stop eager executives from trying to shortcut the process by making financial deals (BDAs) to buy what they think are leaders (but who are actually some of the dinosaurs and zombies we discussed earlier). Sometimes these executives are dinosaurs themselves, so they don't understand this practice won't work in today's market environment. More often, however, these executives are new to the industry and don't have enough experience to know the dangers of what they are doing. In either case, you need to protect your team from the collateral damage.

A Situation Where BDAs Actually Make Sense

Let's suppose Jimmy is an honest, hardworking distributor in another company. He's taken all the right actions, built a nice little team, and has a residual income of 200K a year. Something changes that threatens his future or causes him to be unable to stay with that company. Maybe his sponsor turns out to be a terrorist and is pirating his people from him, or a bad change in the comp plan ends up destroying the business, or the company is sold to a new owner who is a sociopath. Jimmy needs a new home, and quick.

If you're approached by Jimmy and can determine that he really is a solid performer who is being compromised by circumstances outside his control, it could make sense for your company to offer him a BDA. This arrangement would allow him to remain financially solvent while he starts over with your company. It's a win-win scenario because Jimmy won't be afraid to make a move with no safety net and your company is able to land a proven leader.

In situations like this, the best arrangement is usually what's referred to as a runway or bridge deal. Jimmy follows the exact same comp plan as everyone else in the company, but he is guaranteed an additional supplement to bridge the transition from one company to another. This bridge agreement has a runway of a certain number of months, usually six to nine. It's designed with a "top-up" mechanism. This means that during the length of the runway, the company will top up Jimmy's income— from what his actual rank and bonus check qualify him for—to an agreed-upon ceiling. (This ceiling is usually the amount of the check the distributor is leaving behind.)

As an example, let's suppose Jimmy is earning 15K a month in his old company. The new company would top up the difference between what Jimmy is earning and

15K. If he earns 5K, he is topped up with 10K additional. When his new check gets to 8K, he receives a 7K top-up. When he earns 10K, he receives a 5K top-up, and so on. Top-up arrangements like these can bring some great and talented people to the company when the situation warrants it.

But, more often, these BDAs are company killers, because the people receiving them are dinosaurs and zombies, simply exploiting a naive or uninformed corporate team.

As you now know, the zombies have no loyalty to anything but their own bonus check. And time has passed by the dinosaurs, so they're anxiously looking for how to become relevant and dial up their low level of earning. Both the zombies and dinosaurs have been desperately attempting to manipulate themselves into situations where they can receive some kind of BDA. And unfortunately, those are usually not top-up or bridge deals. Many zombies and dinosaurs are negotiating BDAs where their compensation is not tied to the comp plan, or they are not required to meet the same qualifying criteria as the rest of the distributor force. Frequently, they are asking for, and receiving, secret deals like a cooked leg, auto-qualified position, or monthly flat-fee payment. The track record of companies that make a lot of these deals is abysmal.

Think back to what happened when MonaVie went this route a few years ago. The company had a fairly large base of people who loved their signature product and had attracted some industrious leaders who were building teams with them. Then a foolish executive with the company thought he could hack growth and go into momentum if he recruited enough leaders from other companies. He started sending his corporate jet on secret flights around the country, picking up leaders from other companies and flying them to the corporate HQ, where he wined and dined them, offering lavish financial incentives to join the company. MonaVie hit that mythical hockey stick growth pattern—and is now just another horror story, another bottle rocket company that crashed and burned.

There are a couple other recent disasters, whose names I won't reveal to protect the good people still with those companies. One is a company that did a strong job building in the United States. They had a great product story, evangelical distributors, and were one of the early adopters with technology like mobile apps. These attributes paid off with strong sales in the United States, which then led them to move into Europe. For some reason, the company decided that buying leaders would be a good strategy there. It wasn't. Growth stalled, their reputation took a serious hit, and hardworking distributors who built the right way felt betrayed.

Another horror story comes from a long-established company with a stellar reputation that was doing quite well with a predominately e-commerce model. The owner was seduced into hiring a zombie CEO who created a spinoff division of the company and implemented an aggressive leader buying program. This CEO publicly promoted the plan in a big way, suggesting it was the model of the future. He tried to spin the scheme as a "free agent" signing campaign, akin to what professional sports teams do. The result: This ill-advised spinoff almost destroyed the original, strong company.

There is a company operating today with *huge* sales. (I can't tell you how huge without revealing the identity of the company.) They were the hot, sexy, buzz company in the States a couple years ago and rode making deals and buying leaders into momentum. And now the only way they can increase sales is opening new countries, because once they have been in any market for at least two years, their reputation there is in tatters.

The zombies and dinosaurs these sweetheart deals bring into your company shine brightly for a brief time, then move on to another company as soon as they can find a better deal. If your company keeps bringing in these zombies and dinosaurs, here are some ways to you can respond:

- Explain to corporate how this hurts the other lines and let them know that your group might have to find a new home.

- Limit your team's exposure to the new lines that were bought.

- Let corporate know that you will not promote or recognize rank advancements of this kind.

- Demand that special payouts come from other company funds and are not counted against the comp plan cap.

- Insist on open-book policies so deals can't be made in the dark.

THE COMPANIES CHASING AFTER THESE ZOMBIES AND DINOSAURS BELIEVE THEY ARE IN A RACE TO SIGN THE BEST TALENT

Unbeknownst to them, they're actually in a race to the bottom, recycling the worst-performing zombies and dinosaurs back and forth.

Zombie company number one offers positions with a cooked leg. Zombie company number two then ups the ante to a cooked leg and a top-up deal. The next zombie company raises the stakes to a cooked leg, top-up deal, and an auto-qualified position. Then another naive owner will come back with a cooked leg, top-up deal, an auto-qualified position, and a lucrative signing bonus.

Here's the worst part about this whole situation: It puts the focus on recruiting zombies and dinosaurs—and takes the focus away from the people who would actually build a strong team for you: the Uber drivers, schoolteachers, homemakers, and the like—people who have a dream and are willing to work for it.

If your company aggressively pursues the process of making deals with zombies and dinosaurs, they will be in danger of destroying the company. If you can't convince them to stop these practices, a toxic culture will make the business unworkable for all distributors and will result in your needing to implement a final solution. (More about that in the next chapter.)

The Company Announces They're Going out of Business

This is every distributor's worst nightmare. I wish I could tell you there's a best way to handle this, but there isn't. It's going to get really messy, really fast. It first happened to me 20 years ago, and there are still people who won't speak to me because they hold me responsible for the company going out of business.

But the reality is, sometimes companies do go out of business. As soon as word leaks out on this, your entire team is going to be besieged by distributors from other companies looking to enroll them. You're going to suffer constant and steady erosion. Once again, the keys are going to be staying calm, controlling the narrative, and staying in touch. Create an emergency strike team of three to seven top leaders working together, attempting to find another company where the team can migrate en masse. (Otherwise, you're going to have chaos, with everyone working alone, trying to find something new first so they can get their old upline to become their new downline, and the organization will fracture and dissipate into dozens of companies.)

If at all possible, let your team hear this bad news from you first. Should the company just make a blanket announcement and you're blindsided, you really have no other options. Roll with the punches. Schedule an all-hands emergency online meeting. Explain the complete truth, as well as you know it. (The owner stole all the money and fled to the Cayman Islands, the courts issued a restraining order shutting down the company, the company ran out of money and couldn't pay the commissions, etc.) Let everyone know that you have formed an emergency executive committee to study potential replacement companies and will be getting back with everyone in approximately 48 hours.

When that 48 hours is up, you better have something to suggest. Or be able to say you'll have something to announce within the next 24. You don't have weeks to work something out. You don't even have days. Literally every hour that passes you'll be experiencing attrition, as nervous people jump into new homes. Once you have your strike team, get them calling every top leader or company exec they know in other companies to discuss possibilities. Try to arrange runway, top-up deals for leaders, and any accommodations and considerations you can get for rank-and-file people. Anything that the new company is willing to invest financially to preserve your team can pay them huge rewards down the road. A field team is the single most valuable asset in the business. At this moment, all those years of work you did building culture and working down in depth supporting the team will pay off.

This is the time for 20-hour days: jumping on airplanes, back-to-back-to-back video conferences, and 1 a.m. strike team calls. Like I said, every hour that ticks by is costing you people, which will affect your income for years into the future. You have to take bold, decisive action. Then hope you made a wise decision.

Next we will look at when the DEFCON 1 alert comes to its worst possible outcome—the missiles have been launched and you're forced to make an agonizing, drastic, and irreversible decision.

CHAPTER 12

When the Missiles Are Airborne

I worked for more than 10 years in a company, becoming the top income earner, building in over 50 countries, and developing a group that brought in more than 200,000 team members. I loved the product line, the people I worked with, and the financial security that comes from all this. Unfortunately, this was also the company that fired the CEO after a financial audit. Because of what the audit revealed, the investors felt betrayed and didn't want to invest any more in the company. The new co-CEOs were great guys and did the best they could in a difficult situation. But cash-flow issues forced them to sell the company.

Things went sideways in a hurry.

The new owners were an absolute disaster, sucking money out of the original company into a management company controlled by the chairman's family members. Bills weren't getting paid, product backorders became the norm instead of the exception, and the field was frustrated, dispirited, and downright despondent. As much as I wanted to be a part of the solution, one thing prevented me from doing so. I didn't believe the new owners had integrity. They lied to me the first time I met them, and there was a pattern of obfuscation and deception from there on after.

One thing became apparent: I could no longer get on a three-way call, a hotel stage, or a streaming online presentation and recommend that someone join the company. I wouldn't be able to look myself in the mirror if I did. I resigned. Walked away from a distributorship that netted me more than a million dollars a year in residual income.

I'd like to tell you that I had so much cash socked under my mattress that the loss of income didn't even faze me. But that would be a stretch. Most humans do as I did—adjusting your lifestyle and monthly financial footprint upwards as your income increases. Taking that financial hit was like a kick in the groin to me. But I've never regretted that decision for an instant.

Let me tell you what I did regret.

Not having somewhere safe and appropriate where I could take my team. Yes, the income loss hurt me, but overall, I had been pretty smart with my money. However, a lot of members on my team were not so well prepared. In fact, many were completely caught off guard with the loss of income they were about to experience. (A loss they would sustain whether they followed me somewhere else or stayed behind, because the new owners drove the original company into bankruptcy.)

Within weeks of my resignation, the old company had run out of cash, and bonus checks were not landing in bank accounts when they were supposed to. Over the course of 48 hours, I had desperately tried to find a home for as many of my people as possible. But having a team in 50 countries made that impossible, as I couldn't find an acceptable company that did business everywhere my team did. I tried my best, but looking back, I feel that I made the biggest mistake of my career. (More about that shortly.)

But from our greatest losses are shaped our greatest victories.

That experience provided so many priceless lessons and opportunities for growth, knowledge, and ultimately, wisdom. This book is a direct descendant of those dark times. It's the platform for sharing those lessons and wisdom with you. And that leads up to doomsday.

When Skynet Becomes Self-Aware, the Missiles Are Airborne, and Judgment Day Is Upon You

These DEFCON 1 situations force you to employ what I call the "final solutions." The relationship between the company and the field is irreparable and the current status cannot be maintained because the business is being destroyed, or you can't morally justify representing the company any longer. You have a team, they're looking to you for guidance, and you need to find answers fast. Because, as Sara Conner (played magnificently in the role of a lifetime by Linda Hamilton) said in *Terminator 2: Judgment Day,* "Anybody not wearing two-million sunblock is gonna have a bad day. Get it?"

There are three possible final solutions. Let's explore them.

Final Solution One: Take Retirement or a Sabbatical

You hold your position, maintain qualifying each pay period, and keep cashing your checks, but you step away from the business. This is the situation I ended up at when I made the mistake I described above.

The new company I joined had a remarkable product line, wonderful people, and a positive desire to make the world a better place. But they simply could not meet the requirements of doing business in the first world today. They couldn't handle the logistics and were years behind on IT and e-commerce. This led to months of fitful, sleepless nights and deep soul-searching. I spent a year in gut-wrenching despair and depression, eventually getting to the point where I could no longer promote the company.

This decision affected my health, relationships, and pretty much every area of my life. It demonstrated yet again the tremendous influence we have on others and the sacred responsibilities that arise from those connections. I maintained my distributorship but ceased doing any more recruiting in the hopes the company would catch up to reality and become an opportunity I could enthusiastically endorse again.

This strategy isn't an easy step to take. But if you've spent years building an organization and don't have another company you want to build at, it may be your best option. Be warned: Some companies are driven by ego and/or poverty consciousness. Since they know you won't be recruiting any new distributors, they may manufacture an excuse to terminate your distributorship. This isn't ethical, but it happens all the time. If so, that takes you to option three (see below).

Final Solution Two: Unplug from the Company and Basically Deal with Them as a Product Vendor

If you are forced to implement this response, you host your own major events, contests, and promotions—and completely ignore the ones provided by the company. You have to set up the entire infrastructure, sometimes even including the marketing materials. It is made clear to the team that the company is a fulfillment warehouse and accounting agency for the team, but the team drives the bus.

This strategy was pioneered in the early days of Amway by the Yeager and Britt organizations. In essence, they said to the company, "You know best how to provide products and pay commissions. We know best how to recruit, train, and manage the field operations. You guys stay in your lane and we'll stay in ours."

Don't expect your company to be enamored with this arrangement.

Most companies are not. Some execs resent that they're not invited to your events to receive adulation from the stage. They're used to being the center of attention and regarded as business geniuses; being kept away from the field is an insult to them. The company has to pay higher prices for conventions, award trips, and support materials for the remaining distributors, because they no longer have the economy of scale by doing things for the whole distributor force.

Some execs will see your independence as a threat. Because your team's allegiance is directly to you, the executive team may fear you as a flight risk. (Which, by this point, you probably are.) They might grit their teeth and accept the new reality. Or they might find an excuse to terminate you and make an attempt to retain your team. If they choose the latter, it takes you to...

Final Solution Three: Quit the Company

If you've ever had a child or spouse with an addiction problem, you know that sometimes it gets so out of control, they no longer deserve your trust. They may lie, cheat, or steal from you. And even though you love them greatly, you recognize that you must protect yourself from them. And likewise, there are times a company simply does not deserve your trust.

This third option really is the only one when the company has gone nuclear on you and you must respond in kind. You go this route only when there are no better alternatives. Example: You discover the company owner is a crook, the company acts unethically, or they are incompetent to handle even the most basic functions such as shipping product and paying commissions. You reach the point where you can no longer enroll or recommend the company to someone you love. Because if you wouldn't feel comfortable signing up your mother or best friend in the company, then you shouldn't be signing up anyone else.

Expect an immediate scorched-earth warfare reaction when you take this step. The company will likely say and do anything to discredit you. They will spread rumors that you secretly were a communist infiltrator, stole retirement checks from widows, or are a pedophile.

There will be people (in your group and other lines) who remain in the company. They may share the same concerns you have, but they are afraid to make a move or think if they wait long enough, something will happen to reroute the company on a different course. Colleagues you formally had great relationships with will view you as a dangerous threat. Friends who split a timeshare with you, sent you holiday cards every year, and attended your child's graduation will suddenly unfriend you on Facebook and stop speaking with you. I mean this literally. If they see you at a PTA meeting or your child's soccer game, they'll treat you as a complete stranger. If you happen to bump into them at the hardware store, they will move away as though you are carrying radioactive isotopes. From their viewpoint, if you remain credible, it raises the question whether the issues that prompted you to leave are also credible.

If You Have to Take This Option, Here's How to Do It.

Note: Before we get into the specifics, let me be clear that I am not an attorney and can't give you legal advice. I will be explaining the legal issues surrounding company P&Ps, as far as I understand them. But neither this book nor I can give you legal advice. Please retain a competent legal advisor.

First you need to identify the core group of people who you know are *absolutely, positively, without a doubt, unquestionably, 100 percent certain* to be loyal to you. These must be personal enrollees for you to do this in an ethical

way. If you have been working closely with and supporting these people, you will know that they are:

   a. Greatly frustrated or alarmed by the behavior of
        the company

   b. Loyal to you and likely to follow you somewhere
        else

Get this small group together for a meeting, in person if possible. Explain your decision to leave, what company you intend to go to, and why. Have your new sponsor
or a company exec available midway through the meeting
to share the benefits of the new company and handle the
many questions that will arise. Get consensus to execute
the move and set the date for as soon as possible.

Be pragmatic here. If you're paid monthly, you do
this right after the checks are paid. If you're due a big
annual profit-sharing payout in three weeks, schedule the
move right after your people receive that. Once the company is aware you plan to leave, they will lock you out of
your back office and stop paying you. You worked hard to
build your residual income. Take as much of it with you
as you can.

You will want to have all essential contact info for
all of your personal enrollees; make sure the people who
go with you do the same. (Having this in your back office
isn't enough, because you're going to get locked out of
there.) Set the exact time you'll make the announcement.
If you want a head start, do it on a weekend or holiday,
when most corporate employees won't be at the office.
This will slow down their counterattack. Once you make
your announcement, there will be no turning back.

An hour or two before your public announcement, contact all of your remaining personal enrollees to let them hear the news from you directly (and to control the narrative). Do not say ANYTHING in these calls or chats that you're not willing to be used as evidence in a court trial. Just assume that when you call these people, at least one of them will be a defector who wants to remain, and they will be secretly recording you. As soon as they hang up with you, they will be contacting the company. (Or the company has already been alerted and has one of their lawyers eavesdropping on the call or online meeting.) As soon as the company knows your decision, they will be jumping into scorched-earth mode, locking you out of your account, contacting your team, and preparing company-wide emails about your being terminated because you were drowning kittens and stealing candy from toddlers.

The person who acts first and makes the first public declaration will own the narrative and the advantage. Make sure it's you.

DO NOT contact distributors who are not your personal enrollees. Doing so will likely put you in conflict with the P&Ps and subject you to legal jeopardy. Once your departure becomes public knowledge, you will likely be contacted by distributors lower down your organization anyway and even hear from other lines. You have every right to have discussions with them if they approach you first.

I don't suggest using final option number three lightly. But sometimes you're out of options, and the best defense is a well-executed offense. Companies don't have to play fair and they frequently don't. There actually are executives running companies today who believe no distributor is worth more than $40,000 a month, no matter what. And they assume if they terminate you, most of your team will stay, because downline distributors are locked in with the "golden handcuffs" of residual income, bonus cars, and profit-sharing pools. (And this assumption is often correct.) These executives actually do terminate distributors when their check gets too big. Some unethical executives or owners will sense that you are a threat to leave because you refuse to participate in or validate their immoral actions. They might terminate you as a preemptive move.

Companies hold the best hand at the poker table. They have a legal department and a law firm on retainer. You do not. If you're earning 10K dollars or euros a month and they terminate you, they now turn your 10K a month into a slush fund to keep you tied up in court until you go bankrupt or die. And there are bad actors in our space who will do this.

My fervent wish is that you never have to use the final solutions in this chapter, especially the third one. But probably four to six times a year, I'm contacted by someone who has been unexpectedly terminated from their company and hung out to dry. Even if the company acted illegally, that company has the resources to outlast them. I hate to even include this chapter in the manual. But someone has to tell you the truth and reality of what you may be facing. There is one bright spot, and it is blindingly brilliant. Because…

YOU HAVE THE ONE THING THESE COMPANIES DO NOT: THE SINGLE MOST VALUABLE ASSET IN OUR BUSINESS

You have the talent and skills to build a strong field leadership team. Once you learn the skills and strategies in my book, *Direct Selling Success*, you have a skillset you can take to any company, anywhere. We can parachute you into a new country, even one where you don't speak the native language, and you will have the skillsets to build a business from scratch. And now with this field manual for survival, you'll know how to respond to and live through the DEFCON 1 emergencies that may arise along the way. So no matter what happens, remember that. You will never have to worry about providing for your family, because you have skills that work anywhere.

We've got one more discussion to share together. It's about surviving doomsday and rebuilding from the rubble.

EPILOGUE
Rebuilding After Doomsday

When you, the sponsorship line, the company, or even some external outside force mess up—team members lose faith and quit. But that's only the superficial assessment. Because here's what really happens in those cases: Yes, someone or something screwed up and caused a negative situation. But the distributors don't quit because they lose faith in the company or sponsorship line...

They Quit Because They Lose Faith in Themselves

Which is why I maintain that the most important thing we ever do as leaders is to build belief. Not merely belief in us and the team. Because while that belief is important to nurture, the ultimate goal is creating self-belief in those we lead.

This isn't about motivating your team members. You can't give people motivation; it's something they already possess. Your team members have energy, talents, ideas, dreams, and gifts they're eager to share with the world. We, as leaders, need to make sure they have the faith in themselves to share those gifts and talents. Do that and you'll be astounded at how much motivation your people actually possess.

That means protecting your team and making sure they know that your group is a safe space for them, no matter their age, gender, sexuality, religion, or nationality. Knowing that you are the buffer against the DEFCON 1 challenges that come from other lines, the company, other companies, any other entities, and even the company itself. You show them that you've done the necessary work, and mastered the crucial skills, so you can help them learn and master those skills themselves.

Hopefully, you'll never need the information I wrote in the last chapter. (And lots of the other chapters as well!) I wrote this field manual to help you build both a culture and a team that avoids as many DEFCON 1 scenarios as possible. But in the event the crisis situations you do encounter escalate into danger for your team (and probably at least a few will), here's what I want you to know.

STRENGTH COMES FROM RESISTANCE

A windmill farm is so powerful, it can power an entire city. But without the wind, every windmill is powerless. The power comes from the resistance. The same way you build muscle, you build character. From the resistance.

Stop dreaming of the perfect sponsor, team, and company that will ensure you never face any difficult situations. There are no perfect sponsors, teams, or companies.

They simply don't exist. Choose a company the way you choose a life partner. Someone you fall in love with and are enamored with, not because they don't have flaws, but in spite of—sometimes even *because of*—those flaws.

You can avoid aggravation by attempting only those things that you're guaranteed to be successful at. But all that really guarantees you is a life of mediocrity.

YOUR GREATNESS LIES ON THE OTHER SIDE OF YOUR FEAR

Smooth seas don't develop great captains. Stormy waters do. It is only when you face the greatest challenges, endure the hardest adversities, and surmount the ultimate obstacles that there exists the potential for you to step into that highest possible version of you.

Your team needs that highest possible version of you. So does your family. And so does the world.

There will be times when half the product line is on backorder, your top three leaders jump to another company, sales are dropping, and the vultures are circling on social media. This will pass.

There will be times when the retail base is growing with delighted customers, rank advancements are at record levels, you have a parade of people accepting trophies on stage, and the distributors are multiplying like rabbits. This, too, will pass.

Here's what won't pass: Who you become. Who you become in both those scenarios. And it will be the difficult times, not the easy ones, that actually transform you into a true, empowering leader.

As you traverse this journey, moving from euphoric highs to devastating lows, and back and forth between the two, over and over again, you discover something quite surprising. You will realize it isn't about preparing yourself to make all the ascents and solve all the DEFCON 1 situations. It's about preparing your leaders in a way that when the DEFCON 1 scenarios arise, they know how to handle those challenges. You become the highest possible version of yourself—in order to help your people become the highest possible version of themselves.

TRUE LEADERSHIP INVOLVES A TWO-PART PROCESS USING THE POWER OF YOUR LEADERSHIP TO MAKE OTHERS MORE POWERFUL

The first part in the process is your commitment to learn: to become a student of leadership. This is the part where you make your mistakes, hone your skills, gain your wisdom—and develop the character—of a positive, influential leader.

The second part is the more important step in the process.

Because this is where you transform yourself from indispensable to dispensable. You give away this gift of empowering others—to the next generation of leaders, who will empower yet others.

I have modeled this two-step process for you by writing this field manual. Because the next generation of leaders, the one that will empower the generation after that, begins with...

You.

—RG

RECOMMENDED RESOURCES

Websites:

    http://www.randygage.com/

    https://leveragedsales.com/

Mastermind Event:

    https://www.mastermindevent.com/

Randy's Online Leadership Academy: http://www. gagevt.com/

Power Prosperity Podcast: https://anchor.fm/ powerprosperity

Bonus Content

(Some important info from *Direct Selling Success* for review)

Objectives of a Well-Designed Compensation Plan:

- Increase retail sales
- Simplify retail earning opportunity
- Allow new distributors to earn some start-up income quickly
- Increase company growth while maintaining profitability
- Reward correct long-term building behavior
- Provide some transitional income to bridge people during the time they are gaining experience and developing their skillsets
- Be competitive with other opportunities
- Provide seamless payments for sponsor lines in different countries
- Comply with new customer-centric regulatory requirements

- Simplify qualifying to empower more leaders to stay consistently qualified

- Create pathways for large retailers who don't recruit to achieve lifestyle awards

- Provide a platform for full-time professionals to create passive income

- Rebrand away from potentially objectionable terms like network marketing, MLM, millionaire, binary, and multilevel

- Design to be complex enough to promote the desired behavior, but simple enough for the concept to be explained in a 15-minute presentation

- Be a Win/Win/Win proposition for customers, team members, and shareholders

7 TRUTHS OF BUILDING SUCCESSFULLY

Truth 1

It doesn't matter what works. A lot of stuff works. What really matters is what duplicates.

At some point in your career, those words above will resonate with every fiber of your being. And the sooner that moment comes about, the happier, healthier, and wealthier you will become.

When you understand the power of duplication, you'll make the breakthrough from being a grinder to a Leveraged Sales superstar. But superstar in the right sense – the duplicable way.

Our profession is filled with grinders. They may prospect on the benefits of residual income and leverage, but they don't actually get to live it. Because they don't understand the true meaning of those words above.

If you run a commercial at halftime of the World Cup, you'll sign up thousands of people. It would work. But how many people could duplicate you?

Many people think duplication is about them and their techniques and tactics. They think they can muscle their way to duplication, but that never happens. Duplication cannot be pushed; it has to be pulled.

You don't rise to the levels of your goals. You fall to the level of how duplicable your system is.

Truth 2

If you "drive" lines, they won't duplicate. You have to build them with people and process.

We can create hype and rah-rah. We can place people underneath other people in a way that causes them to rank advance sooner and without personal effort. But that kind of driving growth by hype can't be duplicated.

You have to be willing to perform the building block actions of bringing people in and training them how to get customers and recruit other builders by teaching them effective processes. These "safe space" processes protect them against unnecessary failures and dead ends.

Be willing to let go of the short-term quick fix and build for the long term. For every major decision you make, follow the philosophy of the Iroquois Indian tribe: Don't evaluate how it will affect your children or your children's children. Ask yourself how it will affect the seventh generation of children.

Truth 3

The closer you adhere to "the formula," the stronger your duplication will be.

So what's the formula? It is a three-part process that actually creates duplication.

Empower a large group of people to perform a few simple actions on an ongoing basis.

Let's analyze the three parts. The first portion is having a large enough group. If it's only you and one or two other people, you don't have enough traction to get duplication going. You need to keep recruiting until you have sufficient critical mass to start the process.

The second part is performing a few simple actions. You have to dial this down to its most basic elements. Every increase in complexity creates a corresponding decrease in duplication. So you want *simple* actions. And they must also just be a *few* actions.

Then, of course, these actions must continue on an ongoing basis. You can't do a blast of energy for three weeks and then go missing in action for a month. Stay consistent and build a culture of consistency in your team. To create a successful business, people must consistently devote 10 or 15 hours a week to building the business, every week.

Truth 4

You can make the best decisions only if you're working from a valid sample.

Pollsters make informed predictions for a large group of people by surveying a much, much smaller group. The key is to have a "valid sample." Meaning collecting enough responses to make sure the sample group accurately reflects the larger one. Our business is the same way.

If you live in Iowa, you may think the best time for a meeting is 5 pm, because the people you know are farmers and they rise at 4 am. In Buenos Aires you might think the best time for a meeting is 10 pm, because most of your friends don't eat dinner until 8 or 9 pm. Don't draw conclusions based only on your situation or worldview.

Just because the first two people you approached about your product line are allergic to soy doesn't mean that products with soy in them are not viable. And your four best buds from high school might think your products are too expensive. But if they're from the extremely low end of the socioeconomic group, that doesn't translate to the big picture.

Don't make any assumptions on anything until you have at least 1,000 people on your team. Even then, be mindful. And use the following question to set the guiding principle...

What is the most duplicable to the most people?

Truth 5

Your system should be based on the premise that all team members practice three actions simultaneously. Those actions are study, do, and teach.

This is a first principle that I mentioned in the original edition of *How to Build a Multi-Level Money Machine*. And it's just as important today. (Maybe more so.) Move away from this at your own peril.

People naturally want to study everything for two months first. Then they think they'll take action. And then they figure that after they are rich and famous, they'll go back and train everyone how they did it. Of course, this works only in fantasy. Because even if it works to a degree (learn everything first) – then the people you bring in duplicate that process and growth takes too long. The time before people are earning anything of substance is so drawn out that your dropout rate increases dramatically.

You make or break your people in the first two weeks. And the first 48 hours are critical. So make absolutely sure that your new member orientation and system meet the standard of having people study, do, and teach simultaneously, right from the start.

Truth 6

Make all recruiting interactions dependent on a third-party tool.

Here's one of the most important things you will ever teach your team:

If you are in front of a candidate and your lips are moving – you need to be pointing to a third-party tool.

Let's take this down to the most basic and simple example possible: Your customer candidate says, "I'm allergic to soy. Is there any soy in the protein shake?" Of course, you know the answer to that. But you don't answer. Instead you reach for a tool, in this case your catalog. You point to the ingredient list and say, "As you can see there is no soy in the shake."

If they are thinking about doing the business, you've just modeled the perfect, duplicable behavior.

Because, subconsciously, they have just learned that to do the business doesn't require becoming a product expert who has memorized all of the ingredients. You just have to be savvy enough to know where to find the answers.

Truth 7

Open people; don't close them.

One of the worst things you can do in our business is try and master closing and manipulative Neuro-Linguistic Programming (NLP) techniques. I believe that Leveraged Sales is governed by the ultimate universal law, which is...

The harder you close someone, the less they will duplicate.

People you have to manipulate or arm twist to join will buy a kit, but they're the first ones to drop out. So stop closing people and start opening them.

Meaning simply present your case in the most honest but compelling way. Educate your candidate on all of the benefits they will receive from your product line and business opportunity, then let them make what they feel is the best decision for them.

If that means being a customer, great.

If that means joining the business, great.

If that means not joining in any capacity, great.

Thank them for their time and consideration and move on. If something in their life changes in the future, you may come back and revisit the offer with them. And if you treated them with class and respect the first time, they'll be all right with you coming back the second time.

ACKNOWLEDGMENTS

You've probably heard it takes a village to raise a child. I can testify that it takes a mastermind of insightful, wise, and generous people to birth an extraordinary book. The following people filled that role with this field manual:

Dana Collins, Wes Linden, Art Jonak, Andi Duli, Hilde Rismyhr-Saele, and Orjan Saele brought the real-world perspective from the field, with incisive contributions to make the book even more useful for you. You guys are the All-Star A-Team of the profession and I love you.

Editor Vicki McCown, who has the incomparable ability to transform a draft from a high school dropout into a practical, readable, and, dare I say, magnificent manuscript. There are not many people alive on this planet who can do what you do. So please stick around a while.

To the crack commando team at Wiley: Matt Holt, Zachary Schisgal, Vicki Adang, Shannon Vargo, Julie Kerr, Amy Handy, Peter Knox, and Dawn Kilgore. This is book number 13 for me, so I've experienced a lot in the publishing industry. The respect I hold for you is enormous, and the appreciation I have for you is limitless.

And finally, to my mom. A single mother who raised three kids by herself and taught me what it means to matter to someone. I am now *very* old, and she still sends me homemade peanut butter cookies with chocolate chips. Which is why my mom is better than your mom.

ABOUT THE AUTHOR

If you want to reach success in Leveraged Sales, there is probably no one on earth better qualified to help you than **Randy Gage**. An icon of the profession, Randy helped introduce the business in many developing countries and has trained the top income earners in dozens of companies. Randy teaches from real-world experience, having earned millions of dollars as a distributor and built a team of more than 200,000 people. In 2014, Randy was the first person inducted into the Direct Selling Hall of Fame.

Randy is the author of 13 books translated into more than 25 languages, including the *New York Times* bestsellers *Risky Is the New Safe* and *Mad Genius*. He has spoken to more than two million people across more than 50 countries and also has been inducted into the Speakers Hall of Fame.

When Randy is not prowling the platform or locked in his lonely writer's garret, you'll probably find him playing third base for a softball team somewhere.

INDEX